First World War
and Army of Occupation
War Diary
France, Belgium and Germany

27 DIVISION
81 Infantry Brigade
Gloucestershire Regiment
2nd Battalion
8 November 1914 - 31 October 1915

WO95/2264/4

The Naval & Military Press Ltd
www.nmarchive.com
Published in association with The National Archives

Published by

The Naval & Military Press Ltd

Unit 10 Ridgewood Industrial Park,
Uckfield, East Sussex,
TN22 5QE England
Tel: +44 (0) 1825 749494

www.naval-military-press.com

www.nmarchive.com

This diary has been reprinted in facsimile from the original. Any imperfections are inevitably reproduced and the quality may fall short of modern type and cartographic standards.

© Crown Copyright
Images reproduced by permission of The National Archives, London, England, 2015.

Contents

Document type	Place/Title	Date From	Date To
Heading	WO95/2264/4		
War Diary	27th Division 81st Infy Bde 2nd Bn Gloster Regt Nov 1914-Oct 1915		
Heading	81st Inf. Bde. 27th Div. Battn. Disembarked Havre From England 19.12.14 War Diary 2nd Battn. The Gloucestershire Regiment. 8th November, 1914, To 1st January 1915		
War Diary	Southampton	08/11/1914	08/11/1914
War Diary	Hursley Park	09/11/1914	13/11/1914
War Diary	Hagdalen Hill Camp	14/11/1914	17/12/1914
War Diary	Cty of Chester	18/12/1914	18/12/1914
War Diary	Le Havre	19/12/1914	19/12/1914
War Diary	In Train	20/12/1914	20/12/1914
War Diary	Aire	21/12/1914	01/01/1915
Heading	81st Inf. Bde. 27th Div. War Diary 2nd Battn. The Gloucestershire Regiment. January 1915		
War Diary	Voormezeele	11/01/1915	11/01/1915
War Diary	Dickebusch	12/01/1915	12/01/1915
War Diary	Mount Kokerelle	13/01/1915	14/01/1915
War Diary	Dickebusch	15/01/1915	15/01/1915
War Diary	Voormezeele	16/01/1915	17/01/1915
War Diary	Dickebusch	18/01/1915	19/01/1915
War Diary	Voormezeele	20/01/1915	21/01/1915
War Diary	Dickebusch	22/01/1915	22/01/1915
War Diary	Westoutre	26/01/1915	28/01/1915
War Diary	Dickebusch	29/01/1915	29/01/1915
War Diary	Voormezeele	30/01/1915	30/01/1915
War Diary	Dickebusch	31/01/1915	31/01/1915
Heading	81st Inf. Bde. 27th Div. War Diary 2nd Battn. The Gloucestershire Regiment February 1915		
War Diary	Dickebusch	01/02/1915	01/02/1915
War Diary	Vormezeele Ferme Du Confluence	02/02/1915	03/02/1915
War Diary	Elzenwalee	04/02/1915	05/02/1915
War Diary	New Farm Vornezeele	06/02/1915	08/02/1915
War Diary	Dickebusch	09/02/1915	09/02/1915
War Diary	Westoutre	10/02/1915	13/02/1915
War Diary	Kruistraathoek Chateau	14/02/1915	15/02/1915
War Diary	Voormezeele	16/02/1915	17/02/1915
War Diary	Dickebusch	18/02/1915	19/02/1915
War Diary	Voormezeele	20/02/1915	21/02/1915
War Diary	Dickebusch	22/02/1915	23/02/1915
War Diary	Voormezeele	24/02/1915	25/02/1915
War Diary	Dickebusch	26/02/1915	26/02/1915
War Diary	Westoutre	27/02/1915	28/02/1915
Heading	81st Inf. Bde. 27th Div. War Diary 2nd Battn. The Gloucestershire Regiment March 1915		
War Diary	Westoutre	01/03/1915	04/03/1915
War Diary	Ferm Du Confluence	05/03/1915	06/03/1915
War Diary	Dickebusch	07/03/1915	08/03/1915
War Diary	New Farm	09/03/1915	10/03/1915

War Diary	Dickebusch	11/03/1915	12/03/1915
War Diary	New Farm	13/03/1915	14/03/1915
War Diary	Dickebusch	15/03/1915	18/03/1915
War Diary	New Farm	19/03/1915	23/03/1915
War Diary	Rosenhill Huts	24/03/1915	31/03/1915
Heading	81st Inf. Bde. 27th Div. 2nd Battn. The Gloucestershire Regiment April 1915		
War Diary	Rosenhill Huts	02/04/1915	03/04/1915
War Diary	Ypres	04/04/1915	07/04/1915
War Diary	Wood N.W. Herenthage Chateau	08/04/1915	09/04/1915
War Diary	Bodmin Copse	10/04/1915	11/04/1915
War Diary	Ypres	12/04/1915	16/04/1915
War Diary	Bodmin Copse	17/04/1915	20/04/1915
War Diary	Sanctuary Wood	21/04/1915	30/04/1915
Heading	81st Inf. Bde. 27th Div. War Diary 2nd Battn. The Gloucestershire Regiment. May 1915		
War Diary	Sanctuary Wood	01/05/1915	09/05/1915
War Diary	G.H.Q. Line Near Chateau I 16.c. 8.2	09/05/1915	09/05/1915
War Diary	Sanctuary Wood	11/05/1915	18/05/1915
War Diary	Farm 2 Miles SE Busseboom	19/05/1915	25/05/1915
War Diary	Huts Sqr 45. 1/1/2 Mile W. Ypres	26/05/1915	27/05/1915
War Diary	Locre	28/05/1915	28/05/1915
War Diary	Field 1 1/2 Mile S of Steenwerck	29/05/1915	29/05/1915
War Diary	In Trenches HQ Centre Section Near Chapelle Armentiere	30/05/1915	31/05/1915
Heading	81st Inf. Bde. 27th Div. War Diary 2nd Battn. The Gloucestershire Regiment. June 1915		
War Diary	In Trenches HQ Centre Section Near Chapelle Armentiere	01/06/1915	07/06/1915
War Diary	Trenches Hd Qrs Orchard Chapelle Armentiere	08/06/1915	11/06/1915
War Diary	HQ Rue De National Armentieres	12/06/1915	17/06/1915
War Diary	Trenches Hd Qrs. Orchard Chapelle Armentiere	18/06/1915	23/06/1915
War Diary	Hospice Civil Armentieres	24/06/1915	29/06/1915
War Diary	Hd Qrs In Trenches Rue Du Bois	30/06/1915	30/06/1915
Heading	81st Inf. Bde. 27th Div. War Diary 2nd Battn. The Gloucestershire Regiment. July 1915		
War Diary	Hd Qrs In Trenches Rue Du Bois	01/07/1915	06/07/1915
War Diary	Hospice Civil Armentieres	06/07/1915	11/07/1915
War Diary	Hd Qrs Trenches Rue Du Bois	12/07/1915	17/07/1915
War Diary	Rue De Faubourg De Lille Armentieres	18/07/1915	24/07/1915
War Diary	In Trenches H. Qrs Rue Du Bois Section	25/07/1915	27/07/1915
War Diary	Trenches	28/07/1915	29/07/1915
War Diary	Trenches Rue Du Bois Section	30/07/1915	01/08/1915
Heading	81st Inf. Bde. 27th Div. War Diary 2nd Battn. The Gloucestershire Regiment August 1915		
War Diary		02/08/1915	02/08/1915
War Diary	H.Q. L'Hallobeau Near Erquinem Sur Lys	03/08/1915	11/08/1915
War Diary	H Qrs L'Hallo Beau	12/08/1915	15/08/1915
War Diary	H Q. Farm Rue Delettree	16/08/1915	17/08/1915
War Diary	In Trenches H.Q. I.31.a.4.7	18/08/1915	26/08/1915
War Diary	In Trenches H.Q. Le Bridoux Salient Section I.31.a.8.4	27/08/1915	31/08/1915
War Diary	La Rolanderie Farm In Erquinhem	01/09/1915	01/09/1915
Heading	81st Inf. Bde. 27th Div. War Diary 2nd Battalion The Gloucestershire Regiment September 1915		
War Diary	La Rolanderie Farm	02/09/1915	14/09/1915
War Diary	HQ L'Hallobeau In Steinwerk	15/09/1915	16/09/1915

War Diary	HQ Caudescure	17/09/1915	18/09/1915
War Diary	Train Hazebruck	19/09/1915	19/09/1915
War Diary	H.Q. Warfusee Abancourt	20/09/1915	21/09/1915
War Diary	H.Q. Morcourt R. Somme	22/09/1915	22/09/1915
War Diary	HQ Morcourt	23/09/1915	02/10/1915
Heading	81st Inf. Bde. 27th Div. War Diary 2nd Battn. The Gloucestershire Regiment. October 1915		
War Diary	HQ Morcourt	03/10/1915	03/10/1915
War Diary	In Trenches H.Q. Fontaine Les Cappy	04/10/1915	07/10/1915
War Diary	HQ. Chuignolles	08/10/1915	11/10/1915
War Diary	In Trenches Fontaine Les Cappy	12/10/1915	15/10/1915
War Diary	HQ. Chuignolles	16/10/1915	19/10/1915
War Diary	In Trenches HQ Fontaine Les Cappy	20/10/1915	23/10/1915
War Diary	Morcourt	24/10/1915	25/10/1915
War Diary	Boues	26/10/1915	26/10/1915
War Diary	Seux	27/10/1915	31/10/1915

MOGS/2264/4.

27TH DIVISION
81ST INFY BDE

2ND BN GLOSTER REGT
NOV 1914 - OCT 1915

81st Inf.Bde.
27th Div.

Battn. disembarked
Havre from England
19.12.14.

WAR DIARY

2nd BATTN. THE GLOUCESTERSHIRE REGIMENT.

8TH NOVEMBER, 1914, to 1ST JANUARY 1915.

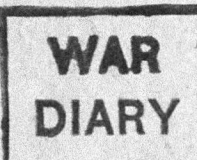

Oct 15

Army Form C. 2118.

3rd Bn. Glouc. Regt

WAR DIARY
or
INTELLIGENCE SUMMARY.
(Erase heading not required.)

Instructions regarding War Diaries and Intelligence Summaries are contained in F.S. Regs., Part II. and the Staff Manual respectively. Title pages will be prepared in manuscript.

Hour, Date, Place	Summary of Events and Information	Remarks and references to Appendices
6th Nov 1914. 9 A.M. Southampton	Disembarked from H.T. Anselon 9 A.M. Proceeded by road to Winchester (2 Trains 3-30 p.m. & 4-30 p.m.) from Southampton) Marched to Hursley Park	A.W.
8,9,10,11,12 Nov 1914 Hursley Park	Drew clothing and Mobile Store Equipment. Bn unrivalled in Route marching etc.	A.W.
13th Nov. 9 A.M. "	Bn marched to Magdalen Hill Camp 1½ mile East of Winchester. Regt. to be in 81st & 13th Bde 27th Div. Continued to draw Mob equipment.	A.W.
14 Nov. Magdalen Hill Camp.	Men granted Furlough 50% for 6 days. Continued to draw Mob Equip.	A.W.
15 Nov. " "	Men recalled off Furlough. Continued to draw Mob Equipment. Transport drawn from Deptford. Boots found to be of very inferior quality.	A.W.
16 Nov " "	Continued to draw Mob Equip. Bn inspected Route Marching & dogging Trenches.	A.W.
17 " "	" " "	A.W.
18 Nov. "	Men granted Furlough 20% for 6 days.	A.W.
25 Nov. "	Capt Wilton Green - 2 Lieuts & 33 O.Rks detailed from Bn to form part of D.o Cyclist Corp. Continued to draw Mob Equipment.	A.W.
9 Dec "	Draft 115 men from R. Scots arrived. Brigade Rt St. March.	A.W.
10 Dec "	Draft 16 men from 3 Gloster arrived. Bn now up to strength exclusive of absentees. Captists Hospitals etc.	A.W.
17 " "		A.W.
18 Dec "City of Chester" 9 pm	Proceed from Winchester to Southampton by road Route. Embarked on City of Chester 3 p.m. Sailed 8pm night.	A.W.
19 Dec. Le Havre 9 p.m.	Arrived at Le Havre & disembarked.	A.W.
20 Dec " 10 p.m.	Entrained at Le Havre 4 A.M. in one train. G.S. wagons to have had very difficulty to train. No lamps obtained for horse trucks.	A.W.
21st Dec Aisne 10 p.m.	General Arm S.A.A. and obtained. Occupied French Bks in Town. Officers in billets. Bks. Batts generally very nasty	A.W.
" "	Capt. - Bks. Batts. Batts. marched nearby H.	A.W.
22 "	Bn Route March Chapman Day	A.W.
23 "		A.W.
24 "		
25 "		

WAR DIARY
or
INTELLIGENCE SUMMARY.
(Erase heading not required.)

Army Form C. 2118.

1st Bn. Glouc. Regt.

Instructions regarding War Diaries and Intelligence Summaries are contained in F.S. Regs., Part II. and the Staff Manual respectively. Title pages will be prepared in manuscript.

Hour, Date, Place	Summary of Events and Information	Remarks and references to Appendices
Aire 26.12.14 9pm	Bn. All companies fitted men to boots over 2 pr socks. Bn. B.s. exercised in Musketry (Rapid Firing) Loading Wagons by day & night. Route marching. Started training additional 26 mm for M.G. Issued for clothing expected by 25.1.15. Prepared indents for extra large boots & 1 pr socks extra per man (make 3 pr socks per man) awaiting Divl sanction to forward the same.	AW
Aire 27.12.14 9pm	Bn. M.O. dug officers standpoints for 12 large shells.	AW
" 28.12.14	Bn. continued line of defence stdpoints in vicinity of Bergarum. Weather conditions bad. Forwarded wire, posts to the heads on firing line. New conditions bad. Boots issued & translator beginning to break up. This afternoon 2 days trenchwork of heavy & muddy I made known.	AW
" 29.12.14	Bn. continued line of defence stdpoints in vicinity of La Roupie. Ground very wet impossible to dig. had to make parapet.	AW
" 30.12.14	Bn. day Communication Trenches. Latrines, Comn Trenches to trenches day in vicinity of Boesinghe. Major Gardner, Capt. W.P.S. Ford, Capt F.C. French ordered to form 1st B.F. immediate Italy. 2 officers & NCOs sent to trenches for 2 days to gain experience.	AW
" 31.12.14	Bn. continued line of defence stdpoints in vicinity of La Roupie. Straw drawn from Birmingham. All ranks completed with translators furs for Aire drew 16 Brigade.	AW
" 1.1.15.	R. Scots attached to B.G. (113) sent to 2nd R. Scots cancelled. Continued trenches as on 31st. Bn. (with B of) inspected by Sr. J French near Boesinghe who remarked on fine appearance of the Regt. Boots giving way tubby, weather conditions bad.	AW

81st Inf.Bde.
27th Div.

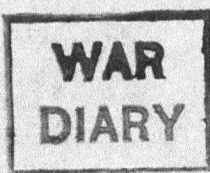

2nd BATTN. THE GLOUCESTERSHIRE REGIMENT.

J A N U A R Y

1 9 1 5

WAR DIARY or INTELLIGENCE SUMMARY

Army Form C. 2118.

Hour, Date, Place.	Summary of Events and Information.	Remarks and references to Appendices.
11/7/15 Dickiebusch Vormezeele	Nothing has occurred on all day, particularly heavy between hours of 2pm and 4pm. From observation our Artillery fire seemed good. Nothing fired caused at nightfall. There was continual sniping all night. Rifle fire which lasted between 20 mins after the At 6.30pm there was very heavy KRUISTRAATHOEK a mile in rear of H/Qrs. Return was carefully run hurridly from any sniping. Great difficulty about water a ration had to be fetched from H/Qrs & ruined Farm. Rum took from 9pm to 3AM. Picket fires were lighted to KRUISTRAATHOEK for water.	(illegible)
12/7/15 Kruisstraat Dickibush	Sniping carried along 6-10 AM. till 7-15 AM. This seems to point to the idea that the enemy withdrew from their fire trench to the support trench just before dawn & leaves in support trenches by day. I reported this to Bde Hd Qrs. From observations from ruined building it was possible to see Germans in rear of their trenches. Artillery fire commenced at dawn. From 2pm to 3-30pm our artillery shelled enemys support trenches & from observations their situation was uncomfortable. At dusk parties of 5 men were sent out to round up snipers. No snipers were caught but sniping by enemy was almost entirely ceased. Have warned enemy to believe snipers are cooks. At 9pm B Company relieved by 2 DCLI. The Regt moved back to Dickiebusch to billets as Jan 7-8-9 Carrollin during the day & previous night wounded. 2. Missing. 5 left to march 2. Arrived in billets at Dickiebusch at 11PM. By arrangements made beforehand everyone had a mug of hot tea.	Persons in trenches unshaven as they sent into mud. Long standards to put bayonets on would cramp this 2 days of trench men must take 2 days rations, if in front line men must Dogrink 24 hours sniping will suffer greatly 24 hours is as much as a man in active up to his knees in water. Allowed up to Key
13/7/15 Mount Kokermille	B Co were relieved by 2 K.S.L.I. at 6pm. The D^n marched* to Mount Kokerville distance 6 miles on men 54 men had to be carried in carts owing to bad feet caused through being in wet trenches. Arrived in Billets line at 11.30 PM with transport & supplies. A large number of men were kept slow up and to bed good difficulty in getting them along.	* Strength of Bn marching out:— Officers 23 - O.R. 767.
14/7/15 Mount Kokermille	Continued in billets line. Get all men except those wanted for march (32) a hot bath & issued a change of clean underclothing at Boeschype. Many rifles found to be damaged due to mud in trenches. (bulged barrel, damaged bolts). Sergt 35 Men run to Boesinghe	Strength of Battn Officers 23 O.R. 727
15/7/15 Dickiebusch	B^n marched to Dickiebusch at 3.30pm arriving 6-30pm sniping started in trenches just after the party. Battalion Billeted in same billets as before.	Strength marching out Officers 22. O.R. 723 A.W. Deary Capt Adj. & O/C B. R.W.

WAR DIARY
or
INTELLIGENCE SUMMARY.
(Erase heading not required.)

Army Form C. 2118.

Hour, Date, Place	Summary of Events and Information	Remarks and references to Appendices
16/1/15 VOORMEZEELE	Bn relieved 2 KSLI and 4 KRR in same part of trenches as held before. 2 Coys and 2 M. Guns in Fire Trench, 1 Coy in Support, 1 Coy in Reserve. Completed relief by 12 midnight. Received 1 Casualty slightly wounded during relief and later 1 Casualty in trench. A certain amount of sniping went on at 9-30 P.M. There was a short burst of rapid fire after then all was quiet. About 9 P.M. 2 & 4 SLR passed over Bn H.Qrs & enroute to be billeted for the night. Owing to fatigue caused by trenches it was decided to have men's packs taken up to front line trenches at KRUISSTRAAT HOCK. Received 3 casualties at DICKEBUSCH.	D & B Coys in Fire Trench. M in support. C Reserve. Pte Williams H Coy Lg. " Attanson B Coy arm " No 7919 " St Enny A Coy Strength of Bn. standing out of DICKEBUSCH Officers 20 O.R. 915 654 not including which left at DICKEBUSCH
17/1/15 VOORMEZEELE	Regimental Support did good work in improving trenches during the night. S.A.A. fire during the morning. Our Support trench was shelled about 11 A.M. with Lyd. explosive shell. This fire was fairly accurate and heavy but ceased about 12 noon. About 2-15 P.M. everything about stopped. From observation enemy's shells shrapnel & Lyd. explosive seemed to be bursting about H.36.c. Our artillery replied & enemy trenches to right of our line were about Christian could not be observed from line. Bn St. Beg on H.Qrs all day. We had 2 casualties during the day * At 5 P.M. Sniping commenced. At 8-30 P.M. enemy shelled over Left Trench. Rallied Hd Qrs and VOORMEZEELE. At 9-30 P.M. we asked our artillery to assist us. At 10 P.M. own artillery opened fire at 10-16 P.M. afterwards given was silent. Regt Sappers worked at improving trenches during night. Received 2 casualties up to 12 midnight.	* 2/Lt F Bendall D Coy Cpl Heale A Coy
18/1/15 Dickebusch	Artillery opened fire at dawn. Enemy's artillery shelled B. Coy from 9 AM to 10 AM but no damage was done. Enemy shelled Voormezeele 10-11 AM and again at 3-4:15pm. Our Support trench was shelled between 1 pm and 3 pm when our rifles were trained to enemy opening fire with a heavy gun which Second shell hit up their firing line. About 6 PM enemy shelled Bn Hd Qrs and VOORMEZEELE heavily. This turned a lot of delay in being relieved by 2 DCLI. H.Qrs 8-30 A.M. our artillery & a trench battery opened fire on German and Casualties in during the day were noted shelling VOORMEZEELE. It was likely by Lewis main Casualties, sniping Rain and Mud. and cross roads at KRUISSTRAATHOCK Our party was harassed through BOECHERSE and the Transport was sent at crossroads at KRUISSTRAATHOCK. The relief was finished by 10-30 AM. The last Company arrived in billets here at 12-30pm. Received 15 Casualties up to 12 midnight.	Killed No 9294 Pte Davison A Coy Wounded No 7407 " Webb C Coy sen No 9285 " Nott A Li No 8532 " Warner A Coy Transport No 9522 " Organ D Coy (Batt Sapper)

WAR DIARY or INTELLIGENCE SUMMARY

Army Form C. 2118.

(Erase heading not required.)

Hour, Date, Place	Summary of Events and Information	Remarks and references to Appendices
19/1/15 DICKEBUSCH	Continued in billets here. Any little work done. Battn taking a much needed rest. During the last tour in trenches we had 1 officer wounded, 1 man killed, 8 wounded, 4 missing and 17 to hospital sick. 2/Lt J. Stall 3 Essex Regt joined the Regt and was posted to B Coy (Major Mills L.O.)	Strength of Bn fit for duty:- Officers 22. O.R. 689.
20/1/15 VOORMEZEELE	During morning B Coy dug trenches near DICKENBUSCH & billeted a gun on his work. At 4.30 p.m. Battn marched up together, the same orders on like personnel, to Support Ypres Q.A. A/ord by 11.30 p.m. the trench, Lt --- --- Support and C in C Reserve. 2 M.Guns were mounted in trenches and by 1.30 A.M. all was arranged in defensive night. Regimental Sappers carried on digging trench to join up gap in centre of H. line, also in making M.Gun Pits in sight of our coast in camping up. R.E. returned to trenches. Rain all night. There was a good deal of rifle fire during the night and we relieved 2 casualties wounded 2/Lt A.J. Black & 3 Essex Regt joined the Regt and was posted to D Coy (Capt Wetherley). Rifles mostly out of R.Belts. 28 men were found unfit to march owing to bad feet. All missing reported except ---	Strength of 13th including O.R. 20. G.R. 585. Casualties No 9245 Pte Woodward B. Coy wounded No 9339 Pte Rigby D. Coy arm
21/1/15 Voormezeele	Up to midday there was very little rifle fire and practically no artillery fire. Weather extremely bad. There was some Artillery fire during the afternoon and a fair amount of rifle fire during hours 3 p.m. to 4 p.m. Owing to wet bad weather many men brought in crippled with bad feet and stomach trouble. We had 3 casualties during the day, wounded. At dusk Regimental Sappers continued work on gap in centre of line. Gap worked hard all night. Artillery fire continued at dawn, 2 of enemy's dug out, & Baganian harassed our trenches from 10 A.M. to 11 A.M. Our artillery failed to bring them down although Regt fired many shells & Shapur.	Casualties No 8840 Pte Slarms C Coy arm No 8703 Gt Denny B Coy not
22/1/15 DICKEBUSCH & VOORMEZEELE	Enemy sheld H.Q. as 11.45 A.M. and it ---- Trench & Support trench from about 2 hours. A certain amount of rifle fire all about. Relieved in trenches by 2 DCLI. Relief completed successfully. 4 9 A.M. in revival, 1 casualty during relief (1 seer 7 BEO 4 man wounded). 3 to hospital sick and during ---- left town in ---- to ---- ---- 18 left to march.	Casualties --- wounded Bullets 24/1/15 No 7423 L/Cpl Fitzpatrick D Coy head Summary Cpl Corby B Coy --- Shoulder No 8774 Pte Hibbard B Coy Thigh.
23/1/15 WESTOUTRE	13th marched out of DICKEBUSCH at 5.15 p.m. to WESTOUTRE (6 miles) to remain in billets here 6 days ---- began to march were carried on G.S. wagons. Billets here very good. Large quantities of gifts from ---- clothing from the troops were issued from these.	Strength of Battn. Officers 23. O. Ranks 625.
24/1/15 WESTOUTRE	13th continued in billets here.	
25/1/15 WESTOUTRE	13th continued in billets here.	Allilwany Capt Adj 2 Gloucester Regt.

Army Form C. 2118.

WAR DIARY
or
INTELLIGENCE SUMMARY.
(Erase heading not required.)

Instructions regarding War Diaries and Intelligence Summaries are contained in F.S. Regs, Part II. and the Staff Manual respectively. Title pages will be prepared in manuscript.

Hour, Date, Place	Summary of Events and Information	Remarks and references to Appendices
26/1/15 WESTOUTRE	Continued in Billets here. Many NCOs & men sent to Hospital with bad feet.	Strength of Bn. Officers 23 O.R. 40878 563
27/1/15 WESTOUTRE	Continued in Billets here. Every NCO & man in Battn had hot bath and a change of clean clothing.	Strength of Bn Officers 23 O.R. 488
28/1/15 WESTOUTRE	Continued in Billets Line. Draft 1 officer (Lt. A.N. Harrison) 187 other ranks arrived 2.30 pm	Strength of Bn. Officers 24 O.R. 623
29/1/15 DICKEBUSCH	½ Bn. relieved 1st Staffords in Bivouacs in Support. Bn. marched out of WESTOUTRE 4-55pm arriving at DICKEBUSCH 6-30pm. Bn occupied same billets as before.	
30/1/15 VOORMEZEELE	Bn. relieved 1st KSLI & 4th KRR in section of Trenches running les by Battn Relief completed successfully by 9.10 pm with one casualty. During the night no firing. No casualties. Killed Friday last night all quiet. Some enemy rifle fire all night. No and sniper and 10 hard posts. Certain amount of rifle fire all night. No artillery fire.	Strength of Bn going into trenches including details of QM at DICKEBUSCH. Officers 21 O.R. 554 Casualties. Rifleman Wounded No 99,16. Pte Hall C Coy left ear No 9066. Pte Rea R B Coy. (through hand) buried at FERME DU CONFLUENCE 30/1/15.
31/1/15 DICKEBUSCH	Good work done during night in improving our trenches and constructing new communication Trenches and making a Redoubt in rear of left fire Trenches. Heavy snow storm during first ¾ of day. About a foot heavy artillery fire enemy shelling our left fire trenches and pts to Coy. 3 shells struck the A&S Highlanders bombproof behind wing burn completed by 10 pm. Bn. was relieved by 1 A & S Highlanders who also being completed by 10 pm. No casualties during Bn 24 hours. Bn. billets to night were in same billets.	

81st Inf.Bde.
27th Div.

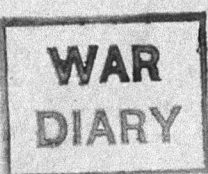

2nd BATTN. THE GLOUCESTERSHIRE REGIMENT.

F E B R U A R Y

1 9 1 5

2nd Battalion The Gloucestershire Regiment.

February 1915

WAR DIARY or INTELLIGENCE SUMMARY

Army Form C. 2118.

(Erase heading not required).

Instructions regarding War Diaries and Intelligence Summaries are contained in F.S. Regs., Part II. and the Staff Manual respectively. Title pages will be prepared in manuscript.

Appendices 7

Hour, Date, Place.	Summary of Events and Information.	Remarks and references to Appendices.
2/2/15 VANIEETE FERME DU CONFLUENCE	Bn. relieved 1st A&S. Highlanders in trench section of Trenches as led by Hem. before Relief completed satisfactorily without any casualties by 10 A.M. All temperance worked hard during the night at improving trenches and making new communication trenches but very rainy and windy. Little rifle fire and no artillery fire.	Strength 1 Bn.— Trenches Officers 21 O. Ranks 531
	Fairly quiet all the morning. Enemy shelled centre of our line accurately about midday. Artillery dealt with the offenders with a certain amount of rifle fire. At dark rifle fire increased and at times heavy. No artillery fire. Working Parties worked all night very hard putting up wire entanglements across gap in centre of line and on arranging trenches with sandbags. Casualties during the day 12 O. Ranks wounded. Weather good.	Casualties: 2/Lt L&AB Laidlaw wounded (hand) 2/Lt A V Blake 3rd Essex Regt (Attached) wounded (Slightly) No 9731 C.QM Sgt. Kay J. C. Coy wounded (Both hands & stretcher bearer sick) No 8764 Pte Fisher J. C. Coy wounded (left leg, slight) No 8199 LCpl Halford. C Coy wounded by slight.
4/2/15 EIZENWALLEE 4/5/2/15	Very heavy artillery fire all day. Our left section of trenches heavily shelled during 11 AM to 2 PM. Bn. Hd. Qrs. shelled at 12.30 PM. 3 shells shaking the farm considerably. Colour enamel of attr rifle for all day. Heavy hostile artillery crashed during the day. One shrapnel burst on our B2 Hd Qrs. Very heavy rifle fire from our left and 4.15 PM leading for 1 hour Afterwards slackened to an attack by enemy into trenches. This was afterwards taken by Infantry when heavy rifle fire from friends 1st A&S Highlanders at 3.15 AM ordered to stand by at 6 PM. Eventually by 9.30 PM 1st A&S Highlanders ordered to relieve us 5/2/15. Heavy artillery fire suddenly fire all night. At 10 pm very heavy artillery rifle fire on our left. Relief was completely finished by 28th Battn. Co. during shelling. At 4.30 AM. 16 OR. in room of family hut. Casualties during 4/2/15. 10 O.R.'s killed 7 wounded.	No. Pte Crompton D Coy wounded knee (slight) Casualties: No 9447 Pte Gibson B Coy Killed (wounded, turned to officers) No 773 Pte Wilson B Coy killed (turned to officers) No 8757 Pte Long C Coy head (slight) No 9645 Pte Mansfield C Coy thigh No 8036 " Harrett C Coy hand — wounded No 9837 LCpl Ridder B Coy head No 9643 Pte Hay B Coy arm No 9267 Pte Dowling B Coy shoulder
5/2/15 EIZENWALLEE	Continued the day having rifle fire and artillery fire heard at 8 p.m. to our left (m). There was another attack on 28 Div. N. of canal 500x N.E. OOSTHOEK [28th D.J.] but our Trench. Rain all of which was otherwise during night except rain.	
6/2/15 NEW FARM VORHEEEELE Artillery Contd. Rgt. to Elverdinge	Getting to LILLE EIZENWALLE till 7 PM. Enemy shelled B. billets from 12–4.30 to 1–4.45 PM Coy keep 60 to 100 yards short. Still being dropped in and around billets. Result 3 men wounded. Otherwise no damage. Referred 8th A & S. Highlanders from Sgn. Co. ? till 6pm to BR-Clayspit 8 m. Gns. to trees, remainder in huts nearby shelled. On returned supply like major hostile artillery pair. Battn. Casualties during day 1 killed 4 wounded.	Casualties: 6.2.15. 1st Bn. Pte No. Morris D Coy hat killed No 9028 Pte Dopata B Coy ton slight No 6907 LCpl Broad B Coy leg No 9873 Pte King A Coy leg wounded No 8935 Pte Fisher B Coy head slight shell Pt. Butt. Trench. Officers 18 O.R. 527

WAR DIARY or INTELLIGENCE SUMMARY

Army Form C. 2118.

Hour, Date, Place.	Summary of Events and Information.	Remarks and references to Appendices.
NEW FARM WORMEZEELE 7/2/15	Artillery duels commenced at dawn. Sniping throughout. No 5 and 6 Trenches were shelled about 3 pm in front of the stills going over. Our artillery shelled enemy's trenches in front of left centre of our line about 3.30 pm with great success nearly all the shells bursting right on parapet of enemy's trench. Have reason to believe that we have destroyed position of enemy Howitzer Battery which has been annoying trenches in R, with 4.5" guns, old R.H.Q. and the L.H.6 Bn in Chu support at ELZENWALLE. This was reported to R.A. and verified later by aeroplane. Have every reason to believe enemy opposite centre of our line was a front Regiment come down to-day. Return from these lines during daytime enemy's sniping was exceptionally good and to right unopposed number of shots hit his Steel loopholes in his R of the trench. During early part of night Verey lights from many points of BOIS QUARANTE have been lower and fewer and light blasts. Knocked down 3 trenches in one night and at support trench 5.6 Rapid fire, then shooting over here. This was completed by 4.30 AM. Casualties away the day [? recorded]	Casualties: No 933 Pte Fisher B Coy Shot slight wounded No 938 Pte Dyfft B Coy Shot " No 8907 Sgt Cpl Rand B Coy Leg " No 8873 Pte King A Coy Leg " No 8689 Pte Morris D Coy hand KILLED Killed at FERME du COURLEVRE
" 8/2/15	Artillery opened fire at dawn. Enemy shelled our Batt H.d. Qrs at 12.15 pm and Trenches lost in it. Some firing from both lines but less opportunity. Enemy all talk over. Returned 4, No 6 Mylaufum 4/1 completed at 11-15 pm. Reg marched to Billets at DICKEBUSCH. Arr. in by 1-45 pm. Reg and S.6 Bygrave Runner in billets at DICKEBUSCH. All in	Casualties - 7/2/15 No 9441 Pte Gardener D Coy Stomach WOUNDED No 9490 Pte Fowler D Coy Lyfstable " No 10511 Pte Stroud D Coy Both legs " No 9207 Pte Davis B Coy Stream Arm " No 10342 Pte Depor C Coy Stroud "
DICKEBUSCH 9/2/15	Returned in L.A.M line. Reg in Brigade Reserve. Total casualties 3 killed 22 wounded.	Casualties 8/2/15 No 659 Sgt La B Coy fingers wounded No 5187 L Cpl Stanley F Coy Rgt : Strength of Batt 10.2.15 Officers 22. O.R. etc 532
Reserves 10/2/15	B[?] marched out of DICKEBUSCH at 5-15 pm to WESTOUTRE to remain in Divl Reserve. Arrival in billets from 8 pm onwards. No casualties.	
Westoutre 11/2/15	Continued in Billets here. 19 Mtd x men opened Reg from Corporal Batt. Reinforcements	
Westoutre 12/2/15	Continued in billets here. Received huge quantities of gift underclothing which was issued to the troops.	Strength of Reg officers 22. O.R. etc 538
" 13/2/15	Continued in billets here. Reg made use to-day etc.	

A Whany Capt Adj
3 Gloster Regt

WAR DIARY or INTELLIGENCE SUMMARY

Army Form C. 2118.

Hour, Date, Place.	Summary of Events and Information.	Remarks and references to Appendices.
DICKEBUSCH Feb 15th 15 KRUISTRAATHOEK CHATEAU	In billets at Westoutre. All Regt billeted and clean change of underclothing at REMIGHELST. At 6 PM received orders to stand by hour away to trenches attacking our line at ST ELOI. At 7 PM received orders to march at once to DICKEBUSCH. Battn on march by 7.30 PM. Arrived in DICKEBUSCH at 11 PM marching orders. Apparently enemy broken 3 trenches in vicinity of ST ELOI but with his salient. 2 Batt of Regt to move at midnight as Bde Troops refused or dispatch by Canadian attack. Regt to bivouac standing by. Weather very bad. Heavy rain and Snow. At 5.30 PM Regt went into Close Support to St ELOI Section. A & B Coys B & D Coys H. Gun at KRUISTRAATHOEK CHATEAU. C & E Coys at DICKEBUSCH. The CHATEAU Blown up at 10 PM (dead Germans.) No though Army artillery shell fire from 10 PM to 11:45 PM (Germans reported to commence attack at 12:30 AM. Did in our night in place to attempt to retake. No Germans through 10 Durham through lost ammunition supply. 10 when rest Regt attacked no one.	Casualties night 16-17 VOORMEZEELE No 10046 Sgt Bratten B Coy killed. No 9999 Pte Abbot B Coy Wounded. No 13373 L/Cpl Day B Coy wounded. No 9801 Pte Crocker D Coy wounded. No 11393 Pte Green B Coy wounded. No 54099 Pte Price B Coy wounded. No 5585 Pte Scott D Coy wounded. No 5923 Pte Fletcher D Coy wounded. Casualties night 17/18 VOORMEZEELE No 9110 Pte Bentley B Coy killed at SHELLY FARM. No 9385 Pte Cullimore C Coy wounded. Engine. No 6335 Pte Webb D Coy wounded. No 4767 Pte Sodown A Coy wounded. No 9092 Pte Standley B Coy wounded. No 9690 Pte Banks A Coy wounded. No 11731 Pte Houlston A Coy wounded. Casualties Feb 18 No 7032 L/Cpl Jones C Coy wounded. No 9987 Pte Sewell C Coy wounded. No 9757 Pte Shaw C Coy wounded. No 9761 " " " No 9198 " " " No 9199 " " " Pte Dillard Shelly Farm
VOORMEZEELE Feb 16th	Regt remained as on 15th in Close Support until dark when it moved up to relieve 1st A. & S. Highlanders in Section of Trenches at ST ELOI. During relief very heavy firing (rifle and artillery) took place. Parties were held 2 Coys in firing line 14 Coys in Support. Occasional bursts of rapid fire all night but the only bad. No 20 French reported as having had positive being attacked by enemy.	
VOORMEZEELE Feb 17th	Our artillery opened fire at dawn. They kept up firing for an hour and all stayed very light. Rifle fire. During night no break out a new trench for use of centre of our line of trenches. From which ran enemy were way about 200 in front of 26th Div on our left, a companies Canadian brought up in support in to VOORMEZEELE. A. & S. Regt standing to at DICKEBUSCH. Enemy very quiet during night. No artillery fire. Several casualties in New Trench.	No 8726 L/Cpl Martin C Coy wounded + 9030 Pte Norwell B Coy "
DICKEBUSCH Feb 18th	Artillery opened fire at dawn. Regt was relieved by 1st A. & S. Highlanders relief being satisfactorily completed by 9.30 PM. Fairly quiet during relief no artillery fire. Occasional bursts of rapid fire. Regt moved to billets but was on by 12 midnight. Total Casualties during 2 days in trenches. Officers nil O.Ranks 4 killed. 20 wounded.	

A.H. Wiseman Capt Adj
3 Gloucester Regt

WAR DIARY
or
INTELLIGENCE SUMMARY.
(Erase heading not required).

Army Form C. 2118.

Hour, Date, Place.	Summary of Events and Information.	Remarks and references to Appendices.
DICKEBUSCH 19/2/15	Continued in billets here. 2nd Troop joined Rt. Br. Lt. Gen. and W.A. Parkinson went sick to hospital.	Strength of Regt. Officers 23 OR 428
VOORMEZEELE 20/2/15	Relieved 1 R. & S. Highlanders in St ELOI Section. Relief completed satisfactorily without any casualties. Position from 8pm to 11pm. Men were very heavy for rifle and artillery fire over night. Pte was subsequently determined to be enemy artillery. Next day during night all were going in front of our trench, 1 Sgt 3 enemy were out of their trenches. Enemy near No 21 French. Regt were all 3 killed. Weather good.	Strength of Regt. Officers 21 in trenches OR 432 Officers 19 OR 358 Casualties wgd 20 - 3 Pte Wholabart No 6461 Pte Smith C Coy No 9229 Pte Winslow C Coy wounded
" 21/2/15	Very heavy shelling and rifle fire on our left from 6AM to 8-15AM. All quiet during day to our front. Relieved A & B Troops French at ... Our line being then shortened 1 Coy was kept in Reserve at VOORMEZEELE. During night completed new French between SHELLY FARM and ST ELOI and a M.G. put in this trench. Enemy appear to be slipping in front of No 21 trench at various parts of range of hand bombs.	Casualties 21-22 No 3690 Pte Gulliver C Coy wounded No 3077 Pte Watson C Coy KILLED wounded at ST ELOI No 6054 Pte Smith C Coy wounded No 9075 Pte Jones A Coy wounded No 4674 Sgt P.H. B Coy wounded No 9292 L/Cpl Ewald B Coy wounded L/Cpl Moss D Coy wounded Sgt Hamilton C Coy wounded No 8978 Pte Annis C Coy wounded
DRAETBUSCH 22/2/15	Trench duty expedition. Sgt Stinger etc. this am. They warned of Artillery fire. Relieved by 1 R & S Highlanders. Relief completed satisfactorily by 9-10 pm. Cap Churchill Lieutenan Janson from 3rd ELOI.	
DICKEBUSCH 22/2/15	Continued in billets here. Reinforcements from England arrived 95 other Ranks also G. Returned from hospital.	
VOORMEZEELE 24/2/15	Regt relieved 1 A & S Highlanders in ST ELOI Section of Trenches. Relief completed successfully 10pm. A Coy 2 A.M. enemy opened heavy fire on No 21 Trench. This is very bad Trench and is not helped by enemy. All quiet again 3A.M. Heavy snow. Sort of Weather 28/2/15. DICKEBUSCH 28/2/15	Casualties 24-25 2/15 No 7091 Pte Dawson D Coy KILLED No 5201 Pte Grantham A Coy No 9736 L/Cpl Smith C Coy wounded No 7663 Pte Dixson D Coy " No 9728 Pte Griffiths D Coy " No 9480 D Coy "

Army Form C. 2118.

WAR DIARY
or
INTELLIGENCE SUMMARY.
(Erase heading not required).

Instructions regarding War Diaries and Intelligence Summaries are contained in F.S. Regs., Part II. and the Staff Manual respectively. Title pages will be prepared in manuscript.

Hour, Date, Place.	Summary of Events and Information.	Remarks and references to Appendices.
WINCHELSEA 24/2/15	Report same day's Coy down of support Artillery fire all day. Enemy shelled VOORMEZEELE - twenty rounds incident. Snow practically all gone by dusk. Enemy rifle fire on our left appeared to be heavier than usual about 7 pm and again at midnight. All quiet from along the night. No 21 Trench on right but took on trench (wrongly) No 21 reversed. Enemy snipers. Lieut. Stephens shot in trench still very lively with Russ forward in front of 20-21. Brickbarn No 21 looted. Lieut Stephens out all night but unsuccessful in locating works of damage.	Casualties No 9089 Cpl. Phillips D Coy KILLED No 9204 L/Cpl. Clark D Coy No 8414 L/Cpl. Whiting D Coy wounded No 8675 Pte Bird D Coy " No 9446 Pte Dobson D " " No 3164 Pte Spaulding C Coy " No 907 Sgt Wigg H/Wy KILLED No 4871 Pte Goodyer A/Wy KILLED No 8660 Pte Hoults A Coy wounded
DICKEBUSCH 26/2/15	Heavy Shelling all day. Enemy's lot opposite No 21 Trench becoming extremely dangerous. It being within 10 yds of our Trench. The enemy completed dismantling totally silenced and a lot consolidation. Reported by 1 A&S Highlanders who we relieved at about 8pm. Second line to Bogy's Reserve. Casualties during whole time of Trench Offrs Shanice & Green/Parker & Withall 2 Wounded 1 Officer other Ranks 10 Killed 50 Wounded	Casualties L⁺ J.B. Shelley A Coy wounded No 11227 Pte Hitchcock A Coy KILLED No 6190 Cpl. Wilson A Coy " No 3076 Pte Clayton A " Wounded No 9530 Pte Pulham C " " No 11653 Pte Penny A " " No 7875 " Vinters A " " No 10138 " Jones A " " No 8132 " Williams A " " No 9920 " Hyatt A " " No 8485 " Thorsen C "
WESTOUTRE 27/2/15	Regiment marched to WESTOUTRE into Divisional Reserve. Arrived in billets by 8pm. Strength of Battn Offrs 21 Other Ranks 470	
" 28/2/15	Continued in billets here. Reinforcements 53 other ranks joined the Regt from England.	

81st Inf.Bde.
27th Div.

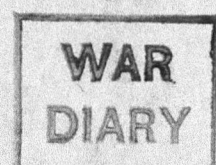

2nd BATTN. THE GLOUCESTERSHIRE REGIMENT.

M A R C H

1 9 1 5

Army Form C. 2118.

WAR DIARY
or
INTELLIGENCE SUMMARY.
(Erase heading not required).

Instructions regarding War Diaries and Intelligence Summaries are contained in F.S. Regs., Part II. and the Staff Manual respectively. Title pages will be prepared in manuscript.

Hour, Date, Place.	Summary of Events and Information.	Remarks and references to Appendices.
WESTOUTRE 1 March 1915	Continued in billets. Received orders to stand by to move to DICKEBUSCH owing to activity of enemy at ST. ELOI. Situation reported normal at 2pm. (2. Batt.n called & issued with shown unidentifying) at RENINGHELST. About 10.30pm received information that enemy had taken No 21 Trench, remainder of Div. Reserve at RENINGHELST standing by.	
" 2 March 1915	Continued in billets. Received information that 4 KRR had captured 60 & enemy Trench in front of 21 Trench. About 12 noon they were bombed out of the position & retired to old 21 Trench. Orders to standing situation at ST ELOI Regt stood fast ready to move all night.	
" 3 March 1915	Continued in billets lines.	Strength of Regt. Officers 21 O Ranks 577
" 4 March 1915	Continued in billets lines.	5 March Strength of Regt in Trenches Officers 19 O Ranks 272
FERME DU CONFLUENCE 5 March	Batt.n marched out of WESTOUTRE 2.15pm. Halted at huts DICKEBUSCH 4.30pm. Men given tea and issued with gum boots. Returned 1st Bn. Leinsters in Section B of Trenches in BOIS CONFLUENCE sector. Finely quiet during night and great deal of work done improving trenches and mounting stores of ammunition in trenches. Some loss supplying them. The Gns W.E. from the two enemy dumps on hill which we are now using as dug by day and was taken by night occurred in saving supplies to all Platoon & Support trenches.	Casualties. No 9735 Pte Wigglesworth D Coy Wounded No 9053 Pte Hopson C Coy Wounded No 15570 Pte Agg B Coy Wounded died of wounds 7/3/15 in at TRANSPORT WESTHOF 7/3/15
6 March	At dawn our artillery opened a heavy fire on enemy's Support line. This was continued throughout the day. The Trenches in front of ST ELOI were reconnoitred by us and our Bn. preceded to stand up enemy's trenches with Lydite and Shrapnel shell. From 6.15AM to 8 AM very heavy artillery fire and rifle fire was kept west of Ypres. During daytime redoubled over the trenches in view of enemy making attack in our Section in a shower. The enemy's patrol completely quiet to our front all day. There was practically no reply from enemy's guns during the bombardment. During the night enemy snipers were very keenly look up. Burning flares all night and occasionally pound volt's bursts of rifle fire for good work close to our trenches along the night.	Casualties — No 9308 Pte Denver D Coy wounded No 8614 Pte Wrigley C Coy wounded at TRANSPORT WESTHOF 7/3/15 No 9234 Cpl Stuart sent to TRANSPORT 7/3/15

Army Form C. 2118.

WAR DIARY
or
INTELLIGENCE SUMMARY.
(Erase heading not required).

Hour, Date, Place.	Summary of Events and Information.	Remarks and references to Appendices.
DICKEBUSCH 7/3/15	Artillery duel all day practically on both sides. Weather very bad. Heavy rain and cold wind. Bn. bivouac relieved by 1st A. & S. Highlanders supported by 11-15pm. Bn. moved to close support Bn. at KLEINVIERSTRAAT, a platoon D at VERSTRAAT. Remainder of Bn. at DICKEBUSCH. During relief there were bursts of rifle fire. B Coy casualties all in No 8 Trench. Caused by sniper in PICCADILLY FARM. Artillery active & shell this farm and about Bishops Hay. But 5 hyack shells into farm completely wrecking the place.	Casualties:- No 7051 Pte Milward C Coy KILLED. No 744 " Lund BRASSPRIE VERSTRAAT 7/3/15 No 6143 Pte Wall B Coy wounded No 9146 " Wilson B Coy " No 8533 " Coden " " No 9019 " Stawell " " No 9212 Cpl Hopkins " "
DICKEBUSCH 8/3/15	Continues in close support. Casualties. Other Ranks. 3 killed. 9 wounded. staying 48 hours in Trenches.	Total Strength of Bn. Officers 21. Other Ranks 802.
NEW FARM 9/3/15	Bn. relieved 1st A. & S. Highlanders in B section Trenches. Relief completed by 11-15pm. 2 Platoons 9th A. & S. Highlanders attached to us for instruction. Germans seemed rather quiet and continually opened a rapid rifle fire. This was probably due to the fact that they had been threatened all day by our artillery. At times there was very heavy rifle fire in vicinity of ST ELOI. Germans continued to carry on work of entrenching down from Trenches and often improved all night. Ram telephones are from 13 Trench. Our Left Trench to ST Mark establishing Communication with Bn HQrs. Communication was also established with 1st Royal Scots by running wire from S.4 our Rt Support Trench to S.2 their Left Support Trench. Weather very cold wet ground. Sniper later front.	Strength of Battn in Trenches. Officers 19. O Ranks 335. Casualties:- No 5416 L/Cpl Westwood C Coy wounded Severe died of wounds 10/3/15 Bullet wound BRASSPRIE VERSTRAAT 11/3/15
NEW FARM 10/3/15	About 2 AM very heavy rifle fire from direction of ST ELOI. Our artillery at 7-30 AM decided to help Bn Bn fire by stay as well as night. Our artillery to our front, with heavy instruction. Continued to bombard enemy's fire trenches and was unsuccessful to our front, with heavy shell burst. In reply enemy shelled Bt HdQrs at 10-15 AM and VOORMEZEELE. All ranks endured to snipe be particularly offensive to-day by sniping and with H. Grens. Up to noon enemy was very quiet. Guns were firing quiet. Offensive in Trenches 8, 10 and 11 wiped over shells dropping in enemy's Trenches to their front from 3 pm to 4-30 pm. French Artillery and Contact aeroplane worked during afternoon. All hypoth shelled by enemy but never knocked but no fire. Enemy being quiet during night.	Casualties:- No 4745 Pte Hall C Coy wounded No 10824 " Clark C Coy " No 9977 " Owen C Coy "

Army Form C. 2118.

WAR DIARY
or
INTELLIGENCE SUMMARY.
(Erase heading not required).

Instructions regarding War Diaries and Intelligence Summaries are contained in F.S. Regs., Part II. and the Staff Manual respectively. Title pages will be prepared in manuscr pt.

Hour, Date, Place.	Summary of Events and Information.	Remarks and references to Appendices.
DICKEBUSCH 11/3/15	At 6.15 PM our artillery commenced to bombard enemy's line from ST ELOI to YPRES CANAL and at 2.15 PM a/c fired 2 salvoes in front of our line of trenches. During this latter bombardment we kept up a continuous rapid rifle and machine gun fire on enemy's trenches to reply. Enemy kept up a continuous rifle and shelled our trenches but with no effect. No 6 pm all quiet. Relieved by 1 R.S. Highs. and regt. returned to bivis. DICKEBUSCH by 12 midnight.	Casualties:— No 8298 Pte Boys A Coy wounded No 8014 " Baker D " " No 3715 " Jones A " "
12/3/15	Continued in billets here.	
NEW FARM 13/3/15	Relieved 1 A & S Highs. in trenches 12 to 8, completed by 10.15 pm. Considerable amount of rifle fire all night. Casualties:— 2 Pte Phillips, 9th R Scots went into trenches with us for instruction. Draft 2 officers & 44 other ranks arrived DICKEBUSCH.	Staff of Batt'n in Trenches Officers 19 O. ranks 463 No 7737 Pte Innocent A Coy wounded Died of wounds 14 & buried Dick Bush 15/3/15 No 2475 Pte David D Coy wounded No 8315 " Anthony B " " No 395 " Tripp " KILLED buried BRASSERIE 14/3/15
14/3/15	Sgt Procter at 4.15 AM to LU off to super opened fire by A & S Highs. About this time some heavy rifle fire heard from direction of ST ELOI. Thirty minutes later all quiet during the day. At 4.30 pm, when 2 very loud explosions heard from direction of ST ELOI. These was immediately followed by an attack by enemy on HOUSE. They advanced in large numbers and our line was very heavy losses. About 5 pm some of our troops 2nd D.S. were seen flying from ST ELOI followed by some enemy who were checked by our artillery fire and rifle fire from trenches 12, 59, and 13. Lt Greenland with a platoon C Coy in No 12 Rot Trench succeeded in completely wiping out enemy who had reached one of our trenches to LU left front. During this period continuous artillery fire, enemy shelling approaches to ST ELOI. Farm HOUSE, ROSSENDAEL and ST ELOI and VOORMEZEELE. On 9 pm Lt Barnsley, ST ELOI — HOUSE—and many trenches to our front and left front. About 6.30 pm received information that enemy in possession of ST ELOI and trenches 15 to 21. Our Buffalo Coys counterattacked, but position 7D & M Coy 56 and front trust of MOATED GRANGE and Redoubt, Reserve H.Co. Brought up to Salient near NEW PARK. 1st A & S Highs relieving H.Q. Subsidiary line in front of DICKEBUSCH with reinforced near NEW PARK. Our continued bombarding enemy all night and rifle fire was heavy between the points front on both sides. EZ BRUILLERS. Guns continued bombarding until getting hot fire and platoons up to trenches.	Casualties:— No 9267 LCpl Donald A Coy wounded " 8366 Pte Birnell A Coy " " 8733 " Steven D " " " 8508 " Overton D " " " 8746 " Beadle C " " " 7937 " Baker C " " " 7132 Cpl Pitt D " " " 11876 Pte Ward B KILLED

Army Form C. 2118.

WAR DIARY
or
INTELLIGENCE SUMMARY.
(Erase heading not required).

Instructions regarding War Diaries and Intelligence Summaries are contained in F.S. Regs., Part II. and the Staff Manual respectively. Title pages will be prepared in manuscript.

Hour, Date, Place.	Summary of Events and Information.	Remarks and references to Appendices.
15/3/15 DICKEBUSCH	At 2 AM 62nd Bgde made an attack to regain Mound 18.19.20.21. Trenches. This was supported by our Artillery who had kept up a continuous bombardment of Mound and ST ELOI from 4 pm yesterday. The counter attack was most by heavy rifle & Maxim Gun fire from the enemy but after very heavy fighting the remaining trenches (19 and 20) were captured & our line completely re-established. Our guns continued to shell enemy trenches at ST ELOI and thoroughfare from ST town every shell bombard VOORMEZEELE and the lanes and about "A" and "B" along. 11 AM 3rd West CHATEAU EIKENWALLEE with some support Troops counts down to trenches about 12 noon. There was notified by signaller Sgt Smith and Pte Chandler who traced wires right up to trenches and succeeded in establishing communication by 2 pm. Y. Here was very little rifle fire during the day. Enemy Trench Party Stationary. Relieved by 1 A.C.S. High. Relief completed by 12:45 pm. Batt'n returned to 6 Hut DICKEBUSCH to remain in close support.	Casualties:— No 11721 Pte Houghton C Coy wounded No 11748 " " " Appendix B " " Strength in Trenches Officers 23. O. Ranks
16/3/15	Contained in Huts here. Draft of 113 other ranks arrived from England and Base. Contained in Huts here.	Strength R. Batt'n Officers 24 Other Ranks 625
17/3/15	Contained in Huts here. Found Working Party of 400 men in 2 1/2 hrs of 300 each from 8 pm to 4 AM for digging new line of trench from BUSHOUSE to S.5. This is a very exposed bit and we incurred 6 Casualties.	Casualties:— No 8779 Pte. Brown D Coy Wounded No 11357 Pte. Fry DICKEBUSCH " " " No 9055 L/Cpl. Batchelor C Coy " " No 8961 A/Cpl. Coles C Coy " " No 15474 Pte. Harris B Coy " " No 2678 " Long B Coy " " No 2000 " Tucker " " Lieut. H.M. Harrison D Coy. KILLED buried at DICKEBUSCH 20th.

Army Form C. 2118.

WAR DIARY
or
INTELLIGENCE SUMMARY.
(Erase heading not required).

Instructions regarding War Diaries and Intelligence Summaries are contained in F.S. Regs., Part II. and the Staff Manual respectively. Title pages will be prepared in manuscript.

Hour, Date, Place.	Summary of Events and Information.	Remarks and references to Appendices.
NEW FARM 19/3/15	Heavy snow all day. Col M. Hind, 2 Corps (A.D) relieved 1st A & S. Highlanders in Trenches 11, 12, 13, S7, S.S. Relief completed without casualty at 9-30 pm. A & C Coy in billets DICKEBUSCH. Fairly quiet up to midnight at time a good deal of rifle fire. Established telephone communication with all Trenches and Regts Hd Qs on our flanks.	Casualties:— No 9725 Pte Swaffer D Coy KILLED (burst behind No 13 Trench.)
NEW FARM 20/3/15	Some artillery fire during day otherwise very quiet. At 7 pm received orders to order up 2 Coys from DICKEBUSCH. A Coy was sent to KRUYWALLEE C Coy occupied NEW ROSBOUCE Trench and S6. D Coy also filled up gaps between T13 and 67 and S2 and T14. All guns up to midnight.	Casualties:— No 7387 Pte Allen A Coy KILLED killed in No 13 Trench. No 9276691 Ammunition Gr Wounded No 11779 Pte Kunns D Coy Wounded No 6337 Pte Fisher B Coy "
" 21/3/15	Artillery duel during day. 120 Q R Scots sent to reinforce us. Then attaching B Coy to Reserve and return to billets DICKEBUSCH. Draft arrived DICKEBUSCH 43 Other Ranks. Occasional bursts of rapid fire up to midnight.	Casualties:— 2 Lieut R J Croft KILLED buried at DICKEBUSCH 22/3/15. No 11634 Pte Drake D Coy Wounded.
" 22/3/15	Little firing up to dusk with some artillery fire during day. Up to midnight there was considerable activity in front of enemy. In order to them up situation in front of Trench 13 where an enemy Sap had was reported a Reconnoitring party was arranged & our up to Support Sap had to wipe it out. Then was arranged to start at 3-30 A.M.	Casualties:— No 2018 Pte Hartford B Coy Wounded No 11735 Pte Landsbury " No 3745 Pte Morle A Coy " No 2165 Pte Bennett Q R Scots Killed NEW FARM. No 8785 Pte Legg C Coy Wounded No 3037 Pte Rollings "
ROSEN NEW FARM 23/3/15	At 3-30 A.M. Lt/W G Chapman and Sgt Jackson crawled out from No 13 Trench and inspected supposed German Sap-had. They found no one occupying them and no Saphad to being an old disused Trench that is probably occasionally occupied and used as a listening post. At 2 & 4-30 A.M. very heavy rifle fire on our right and 1 off our Batteries opened fire. Apparently it was nothing and all was quiet again by 5 A.M. Very quiet during the day. Returned to trenches by 3rd Leicesters (3rd Division). The whole Bn was very late in being completed. Obviously had Staff work on the HAC who should have relieved us in New Barlins Trench had received no orders, consequently what was not completed till 3 A.M. Regt marched to this ROSENHILL near RENINGHELST (5" M.) Accommodation very bad, 2 Coys having to bivouac in the open in pouring rain. The Division is under orders to occupy a fresh section of Trenches.	Casualties:— Pte 748 Pte Willis A Coy Wounded.

WAR DIARY or INTELLIGENCE SUMMARY

Army Form C. 2118.

(Erase heading not required).

Instructions regarding War Diaries and Intelligence Summaries are contained in F.S. Regs., Part II. and the Staff Manual respectively. Title pages will be prepared in manuscript.

Hour, Date, Place.	Summary of Events and Information.	Remarks and references to Appendices.
ROSENHILL HOTS — 24/3/15	Batt? all in line by 6.10 AM. Luther head. 2 Coys dug on the GHQ trench line all night.	
" 25/3/15	in white. 300 men a Coys on GHQ line all night. Casualties during period B. occupied trenches based on DICKEBUSCH. Hope at. attached. Officers Killed / Wounded — 2 / 4. Other Ranks Killed / Wounded — 32 / 131.	Hope at. attached.
" 26/3/15	Continued in Huts line. 300 men in 2 Rshps dug on GHQ line all night. Weather good.	
" 27/3/15	Continued in Huts line. 300 men in 2 Rshps dug on GHQ line all night.	
" 28/3/15	Batt? in Reserve to 82nd Regt. Lt R.M Grazebrook joined.	Strength —
" 29/3/15	Draft of 1 officer O Ranks 293 arrived from England.	Officers 23 O Ranks 605
" 30/3/15	Batt? in Reserve to 3rd Division	Strength —
" 31/3/15	" 300 men in 2 Rshps dug on GHQ line all night.	Officers 23 O Ranks 814
" 1/3/15	"	Strength — Officers 23 O Ranks 823.

81st Inf.Bde.
27th Div.

2nd BATTN. THE GLOUCESTERSHIRE REGIMENT.

A P R I L

1 9 1 5

Army Form C. 2118.

WAR DIARY
or
INTELLIGENCE SUMMARY.
(Erase heading not required.)

Instructions regarding War Diaries and Intelligence Summaries are contained in F.S. Regs., Part II. and the Staff Manual respectively. Title pages will be prepared in manuscript.

Hour, Date, Place.	Summary of Events and Information.	Remarks and references to Appendices.
ROSENHILL HUTS 2/4/15	Continued in Huts here.	
" 3/4/15	"	
YPRES (Easter Sunday) 4/4/15	Battⁿ marched out of ROSENHILL HUTS 4.30 p.m. to YPRES via OUDERDOM - NR VLAMERTINGHE arrived YPRES 7 p.m. A and C Coys and Bn H.Q^{rs} billeted in YPRES for night, D Coy to dugouts Etang de BELLEWARDE, B under command 1st A and S. Highlanders in dugouts GLENCORSE WOOD. B" Bn Relieved Relieved took over from French 17 Div Trenches 67 to 79 inclusive. Battⁿ in Close Support. Grand PLACE YPRES Shelled about 10.30 p.m. no damage done to troops B^{ns} HQ at HOOGE	
YPRES 5/4/15	Battⁿ distributed as yesterday and remained in close support, D Coys Cookers and rations up to Land Crossing due N of WITTE POORT FM., B Coys Cookers and rations to WESTHOEK. wit Bⁿ HQ. 280" NW HERENTHAGE CHAT.]	Casualties :- Officers and NCOs.
" 6/4/15	Battⁿ ordered to take over trenches 26 to 55 inclusive on night 6" - 7". Sent to inspect trenches during night.] Enemy shelled YPRES occasionally during day. Draft 95 other Ranks arrived from England	2 Lieut F. Troop wounded leg
" 7/4/15	Battⁿ still in close Support. D and B Coys moved in morning to dugouts in SANCTUARY COPSE. Established Dumping Ground 100^x S of CLAPHAM JUNCTION and day cookers in Huts. German's shelled YPRES in morning Killing 2 off" + wounding 56 9th Royal Scots.	Casualties No 8957 G^l Hunt Hⁿ D Coy wounded hip
Wood nr HERENTHAGE 8/4/15 CHATEAU	Battⁿ relieved 9th A+S.H. in Trenches 55. 56. 57 53. 52. 57 and R.Hrst. Trenches (81 and 82) in Trenches 23. 32. 31. 30. 29. 28. 27. 26. A, B, D Coys in firing line C.G.H.Q N B.HQ Copse N.E. HERENTHAGE CHATEAU with unoccupied front trench about 300^y in rear good night Enemy's gatling long range Shells of RE. Material up to trenches before dawn	KILLED No 13163 Pte Lomas D Coy
" 9/4/15	Some heavy rifle fire at dawn but very quiet during the day. Our Snipers working in pairs in trees and old houses close up behind line completely silenced enemy snipers and claimed to have hit several of the enemy. Enemy shelled trench 67 heavily about 1 pm and did some damage fire from every close range but unable to burst correctly. Artillery duel about night afternoon, from dusk to midnight continual sniping and about 9.15 pm very heavy rifle fire + grenade attempting on our left Lasting about 20 min. [Ration waggon did not reach Trench up to front has always night high large YPRES, This [R.E. Material] owing to RE. Material being in F^d Stationary owing to F^d Eng^{rs} the peril Germans sounds in this 27 mbent single shoots at T+mpus shrinl [eh 5 stones] [ul 1].	Casualties — No No

WAR DIARY or INTELLIGENCE SUMMARY

Army Form C. 2118.

Hour, Date, Place.	Summary of Events and Information.	Remarks and references to Appendices.
BODMIN COPSE 10/4/15	Continual sniping till dawn. Distinct sounds of sapping under left corner of Trench 27. German Trenches 20 yds away at this point and they have pushed out small sap-head. Apparently running mine up from there. R.E. started counter mining on Pt. enemy and 2 coy digging all night. During the Trench too yds in rear of Trench at Rue Ghelick. Also supported left outpost Trench 31. Counter-mine started by R.E. in endeavour to intercept. Some artillery fire during day. Our men too slow to enemy to be shelled.	Casualties No 9237 Pte Golding wounded 8159 " Rook " No 9637 " London " 12987 " Porter " 9765 " Varin " 6335 " Goulding " 1971 " Burrows "
BODMIN COPSE 11/4/15	During early hours fire was heavier. Artillery shells thumping day. 50 yds new fire trench behind T27 completed and 70 new fire trench behind T.31 completed during night also communication trench from HQ to T.32 nearly finished. Sniping continued all day. About 50 yds new heavy rifle fire about 1 mile to our left lasting about 20 mins.	Casualties: No 8797 Pte London " - 16399 " Godfrey " - 3623 " Godson B wounded - 7398 " Prior A " 1173 Cpl Callaghan A KILLED
YPRES 12/4/15	Some Artillery firing during day. In Trench 27 mining operations started against outpost. Germans seen to be working hard on this head. Contour seen to note Rhine Eastern and west 7 Art men to come out when he was shot and seen to fall up the same ditches as a German sentinel was shot at same spot also what appeared to be a German Officer seen to be hit when he was paid on wk raps for axial commisst changes was close to J. Soppin in T27. Gun may land that aboy 3PM led just trouble wk better. About 5pm enemy shelled CLONMEL COPSE seem of them shells dropping very close to BODMIN COPSE. from Communication Trench 6 T.33 from H.Q. completed. Rifle was returned by 1 A & SH rest of him completed by 1-10 A.M. R.H.R. returned to billets YPRES to remain in Composite Battn Brigade ready to turn on in emergency at Thrown Lane. Draft of 53 other ranks arrived YPRES from Prof. Casualties amount to one of Trenches 1 Officer other Rank. 3 killed. 20 wounded.	- 1605 LCpl Herman A " - 8944 Pte Heade C " - 10808 " Reynolds A KILLED Casualties No. 8979 - 8818 Pte Varvin A.B wounded No. 6333 Pte Harris A " No. 12219 Pte Stratton A " No. 9355 " Yearley B " No 11815 LCpl Sheppard C " " 11745 Pte Clarke C "

Army Form C. 2118.

WAR DIARY
or
INTELLIGENCE SUMMARY.
(Erase heading not required).

Instructions regarding War Diaries and Intelligence Summaries are contained in F.S. Regs., Part II. and the Staff Manual respectively. Title pages will be prepared in manuscript.

Hour, Date, Place.	Summary of Events and Information.	Remarks and references to Appendices.
YPRES 13-4-15	Carried on with line.	
14/4/15	" "	
15/4/15 – 16/4/15	[At 6.30 PM received orders from O.C. Composite Bde. to prepare to move at short notice with 1st Line Transport. Stood to all night. Early no orders to move arrived] Battn. relieved A & H in trenches 26 to 55. relief being completed by 2.15 AM. Battn. distributed as follows. D Trenches 26,27,28. C. 29,30,31,32,33 – A. 31, 12, 33, rif. pt.? – B. HERENTHAGE WOOD and STIRLING CASTLE. Supln. of Coys and Hd Qrs at BODMIN COPSE.	B Coy wounded. Casualty No [?] Pte [?]
BODMIN COPSE 17/4/15	Fairly quiet night. During morning about 7.30 had been shelled badly by enemy and found unsafe, in consequence disappearing [?] Trench and the 99 yds running southerly. In [?] of up to [?] on [?] Stand [?] yards [?] capture of [?] trench [?] trenches BODMIN COPSE 29 & 30 on [?] 5 Att. [?] 7.15 AM we left [?] and rain steadily. No change along our [?] All 3 coys remained following operation orders on Telephone from Bn. Gen. Carton 5.15 h [?] Bde [?] "D" Div will attack hill West of CHATEAU tonight, demonstration along our front will commence about 7 PM onward. Tomorrow to be notified later. Guns will fire rapid bursts from time to 5 min [?] of which Trenches 27-28-29 are to open rapid [?] fire for 10 min, French hospitals. Other Trenches will keep up continuous [?] Guns will then fire another bursts for 5 min followed by same continuous on part of our hys Bty. After that another burst of Artillery to be followed by [?] fusillade. Between 5.30pm and 7 PM our supportion will be up and Coys would be told, followed by a red light on J.5 C.91 and J.35 6.99. At 6.30 PM the following order was received "7.15 PM to 7.20 PM artillery fire – 7.10 PM to 7.20 PM hy.Arty "rapid fire – 7.36 pm to 7.30 pm Art.ling fire – 7.31 pm to 7.45 pm Infantry to cl fire to gradually slacken off. These orders were carried out successfully and at 6.15 pm [?] was from B.HQ. B.M. Sup. 13 Bde. had captured [?] RIDE till 11 Till [?] Guns kept up continuous fire up to midnight. Good deal of rifle fire.	Casualties No 6058 Pte Burgoyne B Coy KILLED No 23104 Pte B. [?] Coy KILLED wound BODMIN COPSE No 12141 Pte Bennett B Coy wounded No 16167 Pte Bellinger B Coy " No 15325 Pte Hogg A Coy wounded No 1932 Pte Walton A Coy "

WAR DIARY
or
INTELLIGENCE SUMMARY.
(Erase heading not required).

Army Form C. 2118.

Hour, Date, Place.	Summary of Events and Information.	Remarks and references to Appendices.
BODMIN COPSE 18/4/15	Consolidated amount of gun and rifle fire up to dawn. At 9.15 AM enemy looked but shewed no 7.30-12-33, firing about 100 shells in rapid succession. The parapet was badly damaged and 7 phone completely blown away. Men were under cover & officers killed & man killed and 8 wounded. Enemy who turned Machine guns onto T26 headed heavily about continuously but causing no Casualties. At 10.30 AM enemy shelled T91 (Trench Support) about 20 shells without doing much damage. As result of this got 148 Bully and 98 Batty on to enemy's trenches. Unable to locate Phosgene. At 4 PM enemy were seen from D we say's Dug out Cap[ture]d Hill 600 S.H. wherever counter attacked. Hill 600 German advance up still about 5 and sent 3 pm our advanced guns of STIRLING CASTLE succeeded in bringing one or he was seen to take down my close Hd German guns. At 6 pm went back with gun fire on them and rifle Ryined by St.R Reg. no. run S. Dev losing whole Confusion gun and rifle fire all night up to Jan 19th.	Casualties No. 15366 Pte Stone C Coy Wounded No. 9637 L.Cpl Welsh C Coy " No. 9713 L.Cpl Hancox " " No. 10432 Pte Rogers " " No. 9695 Pte Cork " " No. 9061 Pte Anderson " " No. 9520 Pte C.S.M. Heyman " " No. 12377 Pte Balham Killed 2 Lieut B.E. Brown " No. 12343 Pte Dixon C Coy " No. 10434 Pte Vick A Coy "
BODMIN COPSE 19/4/15	Fairly quiet to our front all day up to 6 PM. At 6 PM Rt was very heavy rifle fire and gun fire on our Right probably 5th Div front about 6.25 Length on N.E. edge of WOOD - V25 d 49. At 6 pm our artillery continuously opened between BODMIN COPSE - SANCTUARY WOOD and STIRLING CASTLE up to 10.5 pm causing some casualties amongst own carrying parties bringing water and R.E. material from STIRLING CASTLE to the trenches. At 9.30 pm O.C. No.8 Trench reported he had heard enemy's talking at V 26 6 9-3. At 9-45. 148° Battery opened fire on the spot and after what Lieut. enemy's talking ceased. Continuous rifle fire all night	Casualties No. 11880 Pte John D Coy Wounded No. 7165 Pte Smith A Coy Wounded No. 9943 Pte Gilpin H Coy Wounded No. 9084 Pte Parnell H Coy " No. 6837 Pte Owen B coy " No. 6203 Pte Tompkins D coy "
BODMIN COPSE 20/4/15	Fairly quiet during Early morning. About 4.30 pm enemy bombarded YPRES-MENIN ROAD - SANCTUARY WOOD - BODMIN COPSE and GREEN WICKET RIDGE with and STIRLING CASTLE, salt from our left trenches slipped back being however S4 was not shelled 15.4.15. left our whole for from what we could see of the village. At 4.15 pm enemy reached C2 - C3 - C4 and C3 doing considerable damage to accomplish also support trenches and C5-C3-C5 in damage to T6 was shelled for about 3/4 hour and the German artillery fire on our right G2 held 60 from 4.20 to 6-36 pm when Germans rifle fire was heard along 25 men were seen doing clear the artillery fire ceased. T2 battalion rifle fire reached to be in a counter attack by enemy on HILL 60 which retired up to 4 AM enemy's shelled to & bombed the village. So men were apparently SANCTUARY WOOD. Picketed by LT A.S.H. who bombed Company by 3.30 AM Part 2. sent into with Close Support in SANCTUARY WOOD. Part of the Company as others have been saved by the brilliance of C.3 V 4 would Battalion trenches from enemy's shelling. These trenches made in front of C1 enemy in trench was slept all last course of their approach. Heavy fire all night on our right	Casualties Sgt Pepper A Coy Wounded No. 8185 Pte Lucas " " No. 7057 L.Cpl Russell A." Milner No. 7168 Pte Ryan " " No. 9554 Pte Cray " " No. 5354 Pte Bright " " No. 5956 Pte Hicks " " No. 10918 Pte Davis " " No. 1556 Pte Toller " " No. 7744 Pte Holloway " " No. 10552 Pte Parks " " No. 9103 L.Cpl Hinton " Wounded No. 8794 Pte Wilson " " No. 7252 Pte Barnes " " No. 7620 Pte Charles " " No. 11778 Pte Curry " "

Army Form C. 2118.

WAR DIARY
or
INTELLIGENCE SUMMARY.
(Erase heading not required).

Instructions regarding War Diaries and Intelligence Summaries are contained in F.S. Regs., Part II. and the Staff Manual respectively. Title pages will be prepared in manuscript.

Hour, Date, Place.	Summary of Events and Information.	Remarks and references to Appendices.
SANCTUARY WOOD 21-4-15	Enemy shelled the wood three times during the day but no damage, except a man wounded. Very quiet night. Traffic is often under cover from England.	No. 16368 Pte Nichols. 13oy Wounded. (2nd 19-24) K 16.13.1+4.5
SANCTUARY WOOD 22.4.15	Enemy shelled wood at 11.20 sharpest part shifting/ trained at Sp 9.30 AM, 12 of them failed to burst. Attempt to soften sound being to relieve 1 R Sussex in C.10 to C. 18 inclusive. Very heavy artillery fire on our rig LS. 5.05 pm. At 6 PM enemy shelled the wood very heavily. Schrapnel and high explosive. Continued burst of rapid AA fire round the YPRES Salient. Enemy shelled the country right back to YPRES all night. At 2.15 exceptionally heavy rifle A55 (?) and artillery fire to our right front and left. Battn ordered to man Sanctuary intermediate line. At 2.AM Battn ordered to carry out relief of 1 R Suss. who were waiting to move. Owing to Battalion occupying SANCTUARY WOOD [and] the men subsequently cancelled and Battn returned to dug outs. At 12 midnight received word from Bde report that French line about square C6 was broken and full extent there 1000 yards. Combined left Bde full but on account of the French counter attack ordered for direction of BOESINGHE.	Casualties L/Cpl Banks A.Coy KILLED No. 7584 No. 137 Pte Miller C.Coy Wounded No. 16304 Pte Warren D. Coy "

Army Form C. 2118.

WAR DIARY
or
INTELLIGENCE SUMMARY.
(Erase heading not required).

Instructions regarding War Diaries and Intelligence Summaries are contained in F.S. Regs., Part II. and the Staff Manual respectively. Title pages will be prepared in manuscript.

Hour, Date, Place.	Summary of Events and Information.	Remarks and references to Appendices.
SANCTUARY WOOD 23.4.15	Enemy shelled wood occasionally otherwise all quiet. During afternoon enemy shelled STIRLING CASTLE and in turn found to unmask. It was a Dressing Station, a new one being formed at HOOGE. About 10.PM enemy heavy rifle fire along own to front and left which extended on whole 2nd Army front and appeared to be connection with attack to regain trenches lost yesterday. Canadians regained these but on yet no news as to taken trench N.E. by Zouaves have been taken again.	Casualties:— No 5946 Pte Hall B Coy (wounded) No 2033 Pte Slyster B. " No 2347 Pte Coulton B " No 5353 Pte Redburn C " No 10113 Pte Selwyn B " No 15449 " Spain A "
SANCTUARY WOOD 24.4.15	About 4 AM very heavy rifle and gun fire to our front and left. Enemy plastered ground from STIRLING CASTLE to SANCTUARY WOOD with Shrapnel and shelled MENIN ROAD from CLAPHAM JUNCTION to W end of HOOGE with intermittent shells. About 5 AM rifle fire died down to our front in which enemy's gun fire kept our gun fire up. On 5-10AM enemy again slacked shelling forward, until Shrapnel and heavy howitzers HOOGE and MENIN ROAD. From 8.45 AM to 7 PM heavy firing on our left. At 10 AM received orders to place 2 Coys under command of GOC 84th 13th. At 2 PM ordered that Batt was to report at once to POTIJZE About noon 3 PM immediately dug ourselves in a trench in wood in front of POTIJZE CHATEAU on reverse to counter attack on enemy who had succeeded in driving through our front as fairly as Shirley to Battling too. Our casualties were due chiefly to Rattling too. At 6.40 PM received orders to advance to SANCTUARY WOOD and stand by ready to support in event of repulsed enemy attack in direction of C. Trent. Arrived SANCTUARY WOOD 8 PM and remained there during night under instructions about intermittent bursts of enemy fire. AM Guns shelled night falling on our right almost continuously all slow its 10 PM. Our answering to POTIJZE and Stirling Halls and later slow fire mainly all night. We. were. no men at any moment in trench. Guns carried out fire in Chateau of Park by Platoons of 70 man attacks.	Casualties— No 4175 Sergt Patt B Coy " No 8724 Pte Lacey B " No 11509 " Tiffany " " No 16076 " Holloway " " No 16309 " Stephen " " No 6737 " Mellor " "
" 25.4.15	At 5-30 AM heavy Battery fire ceased after fire started on our left but by 6.30 AM rifle fire had died down. Enemy retrieved shelling STIRLING CASTLE SANCTUARY WOOD and MENIN ROAD at intervals all day. At 9.45 AM received orders from 84 1/3. Batt attacked at position POTIJZE 2-30 AM and still proceeding. After a check we were believed to be advancing slowly.	AW___ Cpt Ang

WAR DIARY or INTELLIGENCE SUMMARY

Army Form C. 2118.

Hour, Date, Place.	Summary of Events and Information.	Remarks and references to Appendices.
SANCTUARY WOOD 25/4/15	All quiet on our front during the day. At 3.45 p.m. received following message from HQrs "1 British Bde be reinforced our left, another our centre. Canadian Divn is wearing exhausted & found Divn is shaky on our left". This was in reference to fighting which had been taking place on our left around FORTUIN the Canadians having lost the trenches left fighting for 3 days. At 6.15 p.m. very heavy Rifle and battling fire on our immediate left (28th Divn) then lulled up till dark when it opened down a little. Enemy aeroplane bombed YPRES all day. There are no troops in YPRES now nor round N of YPRES. GHQ stores removed to RENINGHELST. All Transport etc now was round N of YPRES gone to bridges into YPRES being destroyed by enemy's shell fire. Quiet night.	Casualties: Pt Leaney C Coy Wounded No 9632 " Brooker A " No 16875 L/Cpl Collett C " No 9103 Pt Wickham A No 9041 Pt Mitchell B Missing killed
26/4/15	At daylight heavy rifle and gun fire on chateau at BELLEWARDE LAKE when enemy SOLDERS continued all morning and battling left up steadily firs all the time N. At 2 pm Results of left for Pacifies set up their lined from direction of FORTUIN. At 3.30 PM received orders to move at once to POTYGE. Bath was then ordered of SANCTUARY WOOD by 4.40 PM and when in position holding GHQ line east of YPRES - POTYGE road by 4.30 PM. During the advance there were shelling practically the whole way. Remaining in position in GHQ line till 8.15 PM during which time were considerably shelled. At 8.15 PM we were ordered back to our front and St Julien on same trench topst 1 to SANCTUARY WOOD. D Coy came under orders of 82 Bde. Renewed following was at 9.10 pm for 81/83 N Canadian attack has been very Successful. All French Corps 9.9 being on a position W of canal and infilade German position along past damage. Heavy shelling for all night. little profit	Casualties: Pt Chantegry B Wounded No 8421 " Chadwick B " No 9138 " Leeman B o No 9554 " Leeman B o No 11296 " Legg B " No 10920 " Cleek B " No 9137 L/Cpl Goodman B " No 17473 Pt Nab B " N 9218 Pt Bennett C "
27/4/15	At daylight all morning. Received news from 81 113 10.40 AM his reported to inn hot night between FORTUIN and ST JULIEN - C10d - C15a - C16c - N edge C16d Ferma M.W to BOESINGHE. No1 BOESINGHE trench road Luce norderly canal and when French troops are in position will continue advance with objective of BIXSCHOOTE. Using Divn Inft Bde were brought up to stand by 74734 reported about 8 PM trait the was very fit up to ohark 12 noon with advance of FORTUIN 12.30 pm. (Since their keep up to attack 12 noon find further N (S/659) am ordering them broken their along with R from 81 113 at 9 for of Helegium Drift N of the Roulers winding into postponed till shown underly H's Petrol last final attack was rejected. The forces who had back were informed when the possible French line energy upon to hun about POPERINGHE today.	Casualties: L/Cpl Nichols B Coy Wounded N0 3091 L/Cpl Nichols B Coy No 12368 P5 Gokla B " No 9794 P5 Mylan B " Killed Buried SANCTUARY WOOD 27/4/15 A Wincey Capt Adjt 2 Glouc R

WAR DIARY or INTELLIGENCE SUMMARY

Army Form C. 2118.

(Erase heading not required).

Hour, Date, Place.	Summary of Events and Information.	Remarks and references to Appendices.
SANCTUARY WOOD 4.15 pm	Artillery duel all day. At 4 pm received orders to relieve 1/KSLI Transferred C.O. and 1st R Scots in Trenches C 14. C.O. with 2 Coys in support under C.O. of Gordons (Major R Cameron) of DUMBARTON COPSE. A Coy (Capt Gunn) held the Trenches and 2 C Coy (Lt Greenhead) Support. The remainder of Batt. remained in Support in dugouts at St BAG & SANCTUARY WOOD. About the relief being effected artillery fire opened in earnest. FORTUIN started behind being a thousand yards of Clay. At 7 pm very heavy front burst from W direction N of FORTUIN. The latter about 40 min after which the enemy was seen behind STIRLING CASTLE. Artillery fire still continued slackening about 8 am. Enemy 7.30 pm H.Coys in STIRLING CASTLE. Evacuated in waiting an aeroplane. The aeroplane was seen to fall in direction WIELTROEK. It was assumed that aeroplane developed on B5 13.04 which L/R occupied Relief in Trenches C 9 to 11 carried out successfully without casualties. B Coy Started	Casualties: No 16308 Pte Bruston A Coy Wounded No 847 L/Cpl Jenkyns B Coy " No 15879 Pte Richardson B " No 7742 " Durward B "
SANCTUARY WOOD 29/4/15	Heavy fire during FORTUIN 3.30 am what mild rain shower of time. Enemy artillery fire all obry about 5.30 pm very heavy right attack of St Suber Village about then artillery fire at night guns to the front.	Casualties: No 18733 Pte Fitzgerald A wounded No 12810 " Barton A " No 13267 " Kean A " No " Calkery C " No 18795 " Cook A "
SANCTUARY WOOD 2/4/15	Very heavy artillery fire all morning from Eastern FORTUIN. 2 Coys in on report to Sniddle line N of BELLEWAERDE all morning. Passed over 1st Batt. at 2 pm "lost" for French 5.10 P.M. On right our line completely cut attack and wide aeroplane out over found and we repeatedly shelled on trees enemy. First two Trenches have two gun Stated and attack purposed to refuse to hang Trench hard till morning 1.50 Brigade artillery fire heard from Same Sanctuary Wood afternoon 5.45 PM Colonel Thrust on ZOUAVE WOOD. Enemy shelled at various any mild. All towards a factor. Enemy forming gun 8.1 Its 7 pm French left stopped in all shelter Small of Trench to Coke shelled to front 500 yds. No guns reads C 14a. The right Coy sent developed to attach. Capt Hafford and 54 other ranks arrived from England Coy in Trenches reported all quiet.	Casualties: No 8859 Pte Mansill A KILLED CAPT IRELAND DUMBARTON LAKE. No 1853 McJenkins D Wounded No 7963 " Self A " No 7914 " Ardsey A " Cer 22°-30°14 4.W.38

81st Inf.Bde.
27th Div.

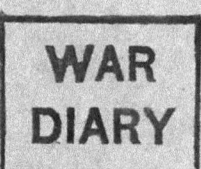

2nd BATTN. THE GLOUCESTERSHIRE REGIMENT.

M A Y

1 9 1 5

2nd Battalion The Gloucestershire Regiment.

May 1915

SANCTUARY WOOD 1/5/15

All quiet till midday. At 12pm our heavy Art.y began to shell TOESINGHE which was in enemy's hand firing over our own 27th Inf.y Brigade trenches. All 19 of Sig. C. 1.5 a/c D. 1.4 Coys 2.1 Worcester shd at D.H. Co. Men were wounded. Sdly 1 stopped by enemy bombarding from site of PG trenches of R.I. SQUET. By 10 pm everything quiet again. 2 German Flyplanes escaped our Archies. 2 Zouaves wood inclusive of shft of Major & Mens Dover two enemy's shots led my attempts, and sound my men in touch of Scot. Household. I ordered that 1. Coys Midlds. R.H. Co. led by my Ground of Ghosh in front. The trench was almost immediately retaken by Supports.

Casualties
No 17414 Pte Dowings B. Wounded Bty A's
No 5719 " Ingls   A
No 8345 Cpl Pimble   A
No 10741 Pte Tucker A

Missing Cpt Fry
, Lieut R.

WAR DIARY
or
INTELLIGENCE SUMMARY.

(Erase heading not required.)

Army Form C. 2118.

Instructions regarding War Diaries and Intelligence Summaries are contained in F.S. Regs., Part II. and the Staff Manual respectively. Title pages will be prepared in manuscript.

Hour, Date, Place	Summary of Events and Information	Remarks and references to Appendices
Mar 2nd Sanctuary Wood	A quiet day until 6.30 p.m. when very heavy firing was heard in direction of ST JULIEN. At 6.45 pm O.R.Scots and 2 Camerons lost two men ordered to POTIJZE. At 8 pm received information that enemy had attacked ST JULIEN but had been driven back [During day new trench completed as shown on map. At night everything prepared for holding new line. At 8.45 pm received orders to hold new trench to morrow night, and to withdraw from front trenches. At 9 pm very heavy firing heard on our right about ½ BN	1956 Yk. from I week.
Mar 3rd Sanctuary Wood	Up till 6.30 pm all quiet. Received orders to withdraw to NEW LINE to night C.in.C. Orders - Sd. Lt Col Gordon Braces Z. (1) The 9th D.L will recconatre the centre section of the New Line as explained on ground to O.C. today (2) Two Companies finished at 9 pm to night 3rd inst (3) The 1st Cheshires and from S.J Sterling Castle to the Trench just N. of CLAPHAM JUNCTION, inclusive will be occupied by 4 coy's (one each of Gloster and R. Scots supporting cos of the 2nd and 3rd French parties have passed N.O.C 9 pm S.H. will arrange to hold the edge of GLENCORSE WOOD till the trenches are ready by 3rd Battn (2) The withdrawal of the Infantry from the old line will be carried out as follows - (a) All remaining S.A.A. Bombs tools, picks, wires etc will be withdrawn by parties from Canadian and support companies immediately approach and carried to the Brigade Advance Depot in Sanctuary Wood. (b) The first small parties - ½ the men in Canada will begin to withdraw at 10-30 pm and go alone to Bivouacs in SANCTUARY WOOD (c) Small French party - ½ the remainder will withdraw at 12 o'clock as above (d) The remainder the 3rd French party will withdraw from the trenches leaving 10 of men with flares in each trench. This movement will be done in conjunction with 10th Bde and will be completed by 1.30 am. The 2nd of the 9th A.S.H. meeting at the same time as the right

(73989) W4141—463. 400,000. 9/14. H.&J.Ltd. Forms/C. 2118/10.

WAR DIARY or INTELLIGENCE SUMMARY

Army Form C. 2118.

(Erase heading not required.)

Instructions regarding War Diaries and Intelligence Summaries are contained in F. S. Regs., Part II. and the Staff Manual respectively. Title pages will be prepared in manuscript.

Hour, Date, Place	Summary of Events and Information	Remarks and references to Appendices
May 3 SANCTUARY WOOD	1. A & C 80th Bde. 30 men with flares will be left in each trench who will withdraw by 1.15am. (2) The 8th & 9th A.S.H. will help in consolidating trench with the rest Battn 81st I.Bde. on his left. The 9th & 10th Bde. are to take the line trench L1 – N. of POLYGONE WOOD at 11pm and leaving this line at 10.30pm. The 1st French Party, 80th Bde. parties, the Somme bent out at 10.30pm and leaving at 12 midnight. The 3rd French Party 80th Bde. begin to leave the trenches on his left at 11 midnight and leave the same line in connection with the 3rd Party 9th A.S.H. (3) C.O. Battns will arrange to inspect at once the ground behind the rear lines of each party and the last few men (who will endeavour) to absolute silence during the withdrawal must be impressed on all. (4) B.D. H.Q. during the movement will remain at HOOGE CHATEAU and will afterwards be established with Bde. HQ. of RIEN FERMEE at Sqr 9C. Issued at 12 noon. Owing to 2nd Camerons 49th R.Scots being ordered to VERLORN HOEK at 3pm to support 2nd Brigade had been attacked there it was decided that 9th A.S.H. replacing the 10th promptly relieved by 9th R. Scots and 1 Coy R.S.R. and 1 Coy 1st R. Scots the Bn is holding 1st Camerons. Another allocation was in progress with 5th Bde. 2nd French and now Battn will move at same hour 12 midnight. Leave Bde. men in each trench with flares at 12.15am. This withdrawal was carried out very successfully. By D Coy of 8th West 2nd SANCTUARY WOOD occupied by French. A withdrawn from all line of trenches back to ling in SANCTUARY WOOD and C Coy in support. Bde H.Q. as shown on map.	
May 4 SANCTUARY WOOD	The withdrawal was complete by 1am and Telephones were complete to the trenches. The new line being continuous. It was sufficient. About 8am an enemy report of the enemy advancing in 2 & 3" At 7pm their orders to serve in STIRLING CASTLE in parties.	

WAR DIARY or INTELLIGENCE SUMMARY.

(Erase heading not required.)

Army Form C. 2118.

Hour, Date, Place	Summary of Events and Information	Remarks and references to Appendices
May 4th SANCTUARY WOOD	4/15 a 20. Weapons at once opened fire on ley M. Guns, after which they dispersed and commenced digging themselves in. Parties of enemy attempted to double across from BODMIN COPSE to STIRLING CASTLE but these had several casualties and were forced to retire. Enemy lay 3 ammunition rows to dugouts themselves in on line behind GREEN JACKET RIDE from BODMIN COPSE to STIRLING CASTLE. About 10 a.m. enemy shelled the front of SANCTUARY WOOD with shrapnel & H.E. 5" hows. They also did considerable damage to our advance trench, with trench mortar which it was thought they had got into position at apex 2nd and STIRLING CASTLE. About 2.30 p.m. enemy commenced to mass troops on both J3. d. & c. at the same time O.P. & trenches were badly shelled. Although fearing of enemy was as follows – enemy was partially occupied and in entrenching a position N.W. CLONMELL COPSE – GREEN JACKET RIDE – STIRLING CASTLE – CLAPHAM JUNCTION and parties have been seen near WESTHOEK. Machine Guns located in BODMIN COPSE in wood J13 d. 4.5 and 2 horse ends of BLUE ROAD J13 a. 9.2 North of road.	
5th May SANCTUARY WOOD	At dawn enemy started shelling heavily on advance trenches and our left trenches and also shelled all SANCTUARY WOOD. This was on till 11 a.m. when the shelling slackened a little. At 12 noon shelling started again with renewed vigour. Enemy heavy guns was causing casualties and worked nearly all machine gun in right front cross of WOOD. At 1 p.m. received following from Bde. "Enemy has made 2 four. Will be under cover on getting 500 and as many of against trenches I.34 + I.33 a Reinforcements have been sent up. 2 Commrs will work all men to keep provisions up." About 3pm received following from 9th S.B. "Enemy parties of Germans are believed to have penetrated B. Ble. Line or are right in square I 34 d. 4.2. 2 Coys W. Yorks to be attempting to cut wires in front of 82 Bde Line. Send I 34 d. 4.2. 2 Coys K.O.Y.L.I. who are in close support to 82 Bde have moved to the right of 82 Bde Line, remaining 2 Coys are in dugouts I 34 d. SANCTUARY WOOD. 2 Coys Cambridgeshires	

WAR DIARY or INTELLIGENCE SUMMARY

Army Form C. 2118.

(Erase heading not required.)

Instructions regarding War Diaries and Intelligence Summaries are contained in F.S. Regs., Part II. and the Staff Manual respectively. Title pages will be prepared in manuscript.

Hour, Date, Place	Summary of Events and Information	Remarks and references to Appendices
5th Nov. SANCTUARY WOOD	Our bivs in SANCTUARY WOOD and 2 in MAPLE COPSE I.33.c. In event of S.O.S. assistance to 9" A.S.H. may be sent to support them. About 12.30 pm when enemy's shelling was at its worst they dropped some light "balloons" right in A Coys bivouac lines. Great damage. Their bombardment ceased about 3 pm but started again at 9 pm after it continued till 7 am. About 10 pm there was cracked .65 firing on our right. Relieved 2 Coys Gordons. During daytime DRESSING STATION got badly shelled and in consequence it was moved to a dugout in ZOUAVE WOOD. Bn reconnaissance made. It appears enemy are entrenched in line as shewn on map. Enemy's aircraft very busy all day	
6 Nov. SANCTUARY WOOD	At 9 am enemy started bombarding our trenches and the Wood again. Our two Field Kitchens and enemy's guns ceased firing. All M.Gs are concentrated again but at about 2.30 A.M. Our 9.2 Hows strafed & opened fire on BODMIN COPSE and STRONG POINT during the afternoon with some effect. German snipers much more active to day probably because Regt have finished digging themselves in. Enemy fairly quiet during afternoon up to midnight. Their reconnaissance enemy have advanced their trenches in front BODMIN COPSE to in front of STIRLING CASTLE. Probably in front STIRLING CASTLE greatly in lands. About 10.5 there was a heavy rapid fire on our right but it proved to be nothing. Received information that S'.A'res in possession will be.	
7 Nov SANCTUARY WOOD	About 5.30 am on M.G. on left corner of advance trench across the whole of our front causing rapid fire for 15 mins from German & British for half or so each side of our lines. About 8 am our heavy rifle & artillery fire & and 600 to our left also opened up on our lines. led by 4 am it had practically ceased. At 10.45 enemy commenced shelling our trenches & dugouts again During night enemy have constructed a small advance trench about 100 x N.W. Inner Ays. Heavy artillery fire all day both from us more enemy's guns. Our guns seemed to get the upper hand to day and consequently	

INTELLIGENCE SUMMARY / WAR DIARY

Army Form C. 2118.

Instructions regarding War Diaries and Intelligence Summaries are contained in F.S. Regs., Part II and the Staff Manual respectively. Title pages will be prepared in manuscript.

(Erase heading not required.)

Hour, Date, Place	Summary of Events and Information	Remarks and references to Appendices
7th May SANCTUARY WOOD	We have comparatively small casualties. Casualties during day very small estates owing to continued bombardment beyond ground, where shooting was excelled from reconnaissances made. Enemy have started new ground which runs from S.E. corner of WOOD JA 4.7.7. to encroache 19a. Enemy seen to be seen this end at dusk and 1 man carrying plank seen out of trench to work to the rear but unmolested over 6.3. 2 shots fired by observer from 19a. Bj. 5. The men doubtless uniform with army pennicap. Those say he was lancer Coy. All enemy trenches are new loopholed every few yards.	
8th May SANCTUARY WOOD	CO went up to trenches when enemy bombarded our right trench and trench in from 11 a.m. Received information that enemy had broken through at BELLEWARDE LAKE. This was subsequently known at 14.12 under enemy 1812½. bombarding our trenches and supports furiously. At 1pm Capt Rupp (C. & C.) in advance French reported 2 more heavy heavy casualties and was only holding advance French lightly. Remainder of his Coy. were in the French trench. At 3pm I Bourts enemy shelling increased and at 3.30 pm things got so bad that CO decided to reinforce. Left Coy (C) with the support Coy (B) and brought Reserve Coy (D) to line trenches and 2 Coy Lancasts which are supporting us were brought up to Reserve Coy dugouts. At 4.30 pm enemy shell fire quieted down considerably and C.O decided to withdraw reserves. Reserve Coy and sent back 2 Coys Lancasts trying to break at front of BELLEWARDE M.A.S.H. even kept up supply fire all day and night F 4.9. Alph 4. Ypres enemy kept up heavy bombardment of our trenches causing heavy casualties and damages to parapet. At 6 am enemy opened with rapid rifle fire 12.0 to midnight after Rush considerable amount of rifle fire and one night of trench. At Guns opened, also a certain amount of artillery fire.	

INTELLIGENCE SUMMARY

(Erase heading not required.)

Instructions regarding War Diaries and Intelligence Summaries are contained in F.S. Regs., Part II and the Staff Manual respectively. Title pages will be prepared in manuscript.

Hour, Date, Place	Summary of Events and Information	Remarks and references to Appendices
July / SANCTUARY WOOD	The Battn held following position of attack. Sketch B. B Co. under Major Nisbet holding left half of the trenches excluding Advanced Trench. D Co. under R. Gradbrook holding right half of trenches. A Coy was in close support behind B Coy. to Coy. in Reserve at Balm. H.Q. He attached sketch. He advanced trench was held as follows: 1 Platoon under J Deplin left front of trench. 1 Platoon under Sgt. Copley right front of trench. 1 Platoon under Sgt. Bull right flank of trench. 1 hour after dawn troops held retired each of these platoons, Sgt. Bull's right flank to reduce their numbers by ½ and send them back to Main Trench. At 5.30 am enemy opened with heavy artillery fire on our trenches more especially the advanced Trench. This lasted for 10 minutes when they opened rank very heavy rifle fire. Rifle fire... they ceased again with artillery fire lasting for 10 mins. As a result of the great damage was done to the parapet and it was discovered Lt. Deplin & his platoon was completely cut off, owing to a large bit of the trench being blown in. Major Nisbet also seeing it was getting heavy casualties ordered the 3 Platoons on the advanced Trench to reduce to 10 men per platoon. On top of the heavy shelling the enemy again opened with rapid fire for 15 mins followed by terrific artillery fire for 10 mins. At 7.15am enemy attacked advancing from STIRLING CASTLE - and our right front. Although heavy fire was brought to bear on them from Sgt. Bull & Platoon and M.G. the enemy succeeded in gaining trenches (marked) 142 on map and commanded the trenches. It afterwards transpired that Lt. Deplin at the time badly wounded, during the 3rd shelling had withdrawn with 3 men to Main Trench having found her bit of Advanced Trench untenable, and that Sgt. Copley with two fire men after the 3rd shelling were completely cut off from their right by the French being driven away. About 7.25 am enemy got into the left corner and in front of 3, commenced digging themselves in. Their losses here were severe also on the left, estimated about 350 killed. At 7.30 am	No. 12 Pte. Hancock Killed Corp. Wood Missing 1534 Davis "

Instructions regarding War Diaries and Intelligence Summaries are contained in F.S. Regs., Part II. and the Staff Manual respectively. Title pages will be prepared in manuscript.

INTELLIGENCE SUMMARY.

(Erase heading not required.)

Army Form C. 2118.

Hour, Date, Place	Summary of Events and Information	Remarks and references to Appendices
May 9. SANCTUARY WOOD	enemy came be seen on Y but fire brought on them from 1 and N°2 MG and enfilade sniping from B. They commenced to retire about 7.50 a.m. Here again they lost fairly heavily as the 2 M.G. were able to open fire. The 1st news of the attack was received at H.Q. by runner (The telephone having been smashed to bits by enemy's shell fire) at 7.20 a.m. The support Company with 2ⁿᵈ C Major Conran was rushed into the main Trench to meet the attack. Apparently Major Conran advanced with some men from 2 and drove enemy up to the corner of D but eventually was overpowered and he and his party were either taken prisoners or killed. At the same time the Reserve Coy with H.Qrs moved to about 250ˣ in rear of main Trench. 2 Coys Leinsters also came up in support, 1 at 9.10 a.m. the situation seeming critical the Reserve Coy & Leinsters retired to their original places. At 9.15 a.m Signaller Sgt South who had been up to 0 to mend telephone brought back the information that the Germans were in 1 & 2. The C.O. (Col Smith) then ordered up the Reserve Coy K just behind Right Main Trench. He then ordered that Major Heath should advance up 2 throwing bombs and that A Coy also send bombing party via Y + 2 while C Coy did the same by Z. This was carried out but owing to the enemy's bombs being so much better than ours, the effort was stopped, and an attack decided on.	
A.H.Q. line near CHATEAU I. W.Coy	Plan of attack as follows 1 Platoon of Major Heath's to attack from 3 direction 2, and 2 Platoons under Capt Spear in Yorkshire 2 and 1. 2 Platoons of Raquet's? direction 1. Each party had 6 men with bombs to go with the attack. Each party was in position by 3 p.m. The signal for the advance was to be rapid fire for 1 min from Capt Spear 2 Platoons after which every man was to go charge for the Germans. The plans attacking farther were ordered to get up one of the Trenches immediately their rapid fire started. The 61st R.F.A. and 75 R.F.A. were to shell German Trenches facing S. around Sterling Castle from 3.15 p.m. to 4 p.m. the attack being ordered for 3.30 p.m. 2 Platoons were kept in MAIN TRENCH as a	

INTELLIGENCE SUMMARY

(Erase heading not required.)

Instructions regarding War Diaries and Intelligence Summaries are contained in F.S. Regs., Part II. and the Staff Manual respectively. Title pages will be prepared in manuscript.

Hour, Date, Place	Summary of Events and Information	Remarks and references to Appendices
G.H.Q. Line CHATEAU = 16 C 5.7	9th May support, 1 & 2 Platoons 100x in rear of Firing Trench as Reserve. They were 2 Coys of R Scots in rear occupying 2nd line. The Cameron Highlanders on our left were to open rapid fire on Trenches in front of STIRLING CASTLE at 3:30pm. This was duly carried out and at 3:45pm Capt Speir opened with 2 men of rapid fire. After which the left & centre parties advanced over the open at the enemy. Though our hitch the left party was a few seconds late in the advance. This attack was met with a terrific fire from the enemy who who had a M.G. in every spot, and 2 mile near STIRLING CASTLE. The ground swing to fallen lases stood like one who was entirely impossible to advance over and being rocked by the Rapid fire the attack got up to 15 to 20 y of enemy does a firing line was established. If supports could have been got up at once the attack would have broken into enemy Trenches but the numbers of ground made the bringing up of support a very long proceeding, and before supports could come the attacking party was practically wiped out with the exception of Capt Rayner who established himself about 10X from enemy and threw bombs into their Trenches. Sgt Baker with a few men in the centre and Capts Speir had then took immense aid advances to Rs Coys, & Sgt Baker to withdraw and withdraw himself to Y. Between Major Ricobet & men in right Coop Henry who was Col Field had been and Coy. & Lt Lyons, Capt Lapt Henry coming to 3. Lt Vicar Speiren & Lt Baker and others, Capt & Lt to hold Y, and if no Fresh and Cemetery to B. Reserve. The position was reported to Bn H.Q. being held by Lt Capt Henry, Capt Speir up of our Reserve. This position was reported to Bn H.Q. there was on the phone asking communication and General further orders no further attack to be sieges at 6.30pm not accompany any definite news as to whether Major Ricobet was killed and especie and or whether his little force could continue to hold out. Capt Vicary got out to him and found him quite secure though he had had heavy casualties. Y (A.G. of action Major Ricobet When assumed command of the Battn and left Capt Seaford in command of advanced trench the position of trenches at this time is as shown of map B. Our position was maintained.	

INTELLIGENCE SUMMARY.

(Erase heading not required.)

Instructions regarding War Diaries and Intelligence Summaries are contained in F.S. Regs., Part II. and the Staff Manual respectively. Title pages will be prepared in manuscript.

Hour, Date, Place	Summary of Events and Information	Remarks and references to Appendices

May 9th G.H.Q. line near CHATEAU I.N.C.8.2.

until relieved by 1 R Scots when we retired to G.H.Q line S. of MENIN Road near Railway Crossing. We were in position there by 3.45am having brought out all our wounded thanks to splendid work done by Stretcher Bearers v R.A.M.C. All through the action the Regt Signallers did magnificent work in keeping communication if any can be picked out it would be Sgt Cullemore, Pte Glassier – Pte Bottime v Sgt Sinclair. Casualties during the day from 1 Officer 1 killed 3 wounded 1 missing. Other Ranks 29 killed 93 wounded 8 missing. Held about 300x of G.H.Q line from CHATEAU to ZILLEBEKE - POTYZE road. Shelled badly all day with small H.E. Explosion. Very heavy firing all day to our front. YPRES in flames. Worked all night at improving the Trenches.

May 10th SANCTUARY WOOD

Enemy shelled our trenches heavily all day. At 1:30pm received orders to go into post in trees found S.E. of HIMERTUNGE. On further received news from 2 J Division & report to H.Qrs 8th Bde in SANCTUARY WOOD at once. Both arrived there at 9.15p.m. Coy immediately moved off to dig support trench shown on sketch. The situation was as follows:- The trenches which were holding for 15 last 2 months A.M. etc had during the evening been forced Evacuate & owing to being so heavily shelled that the French became untenable. The enemy had thrown in large number of troops & had occupied it and also the hill South of it. Two something were made to retake it in the night. In order to clear up situation a reconnaissance was made. All four what it was discovered that enemy was occupying more troops up to the line 2 wounded German were also captured. It was immediately decided to attack with 2 Coys of Leinster. This after 2 attempts was unsuccessful at 3.15am – 1 Coy of 4th R.I.R (Capt Browne) was ordered up to have pass from "W" to prevent enemy coming into his line, not a Captain reached the hill, but the bayonets and drove the enemy off. He then the R.I.R of "A" was during the whole time being subjected to heavy artillery fire. He then decided to withdraw. At 11.15am enemy were seen massing behind hill, and Capt Brown again took hill with the bayonet and dispersed them. Capt Brown decided not to hold the hill

Army Form C. 2118.

Instructions regarding War Diaries and Intelligence Summaries are contained in F.S. Regs., Part II. and the Staff Manual respectively. Title pages will be prepared in manuscript.

WAR DIARY or INTELLIGENCE SUMMARY.

(Erase heading not required).

Hour, Date, Place.	Summary of Events and Information.	Remarks and references to Appendices.
9th May SANCTUARY WOOD	Army 5 Sunners shell fire and M.G fire. Reinforcements were sent to him C Coy. 10 Noon and M.G. At 9am B Coy was withdrawn having practically been exhausted and having had some very hard work during the past few days they were exhausted. Relieved from decided to occupy Hill 60 with from 1 & 2nd line even as he did not intend the loss due to a shelling was justified knowing that loss occupation Shipes & hill of his O.P.s. During the day C Coy assisted when 3rd line in the 2nd line and our artillery shelled the hill, a a gunner eventually. At 4 pm with C Coy 2 line sent with 2 Platoons had a support and a reserve Platoon under Lt Gates and M.G. to close up under the second extending from the hedge on ____ each man of the Platoons carried 1 full reading and instructions attempted to reach the men to get some cover directly they got on position, the attempt being that they should act as a covering party whilst a retrenchment was being made. This was very successful except 2 Platoon 2 Coy (Lt Graydon) some 15 plus, men of 2 line in reserve and Reg.t H.Q. were established on 2nd line. The front was not consolidated before Light ? which we moved to dugouts and entrenchment was reached after dark.	
10th May SANCTUARY WOOD	During May 10th 1915 at [?] moving sniping is done to snipers to support all teams our and night. A number of ____ ____ ____ Enemy trenches be sniped from [?] was _____ the enemy has occupied and occupying trenches abandoned by ourselves on the first. Shortly after this we have ____ [?] the enemy ____ if the corps commander ordered the _____ . At 3pm and cap to about an hour later in the meantime the regulate Establish brigade made to be able to arrange for a relief shortly. The cavalry even left have had heavy fighting near Bellewarde [?] __ [?] Brigade ___ from frequent ___	

Army Form C. 2118.

WAR DIARY
or
INTELLIGENCE SUMMARY.
(Erase heading not required).

Instructions regarding War Diaries and Intelligence Summaries are contained in F.S. Regs., Part II. and the Staff Manual respectively. Title pages will be prepared in manuscript.

Hour, Date, Place.	Summary of Events and Information.	Remarks and references to Appendices.

MAY 14 SANCTUARY WOOD

Early in morning received orders stand by to support 9" Rdo who were desperately threatened. Enemy very much quieter all day. At 6.30 pm received orders to relieve Lincolns in retrenchment & 2" Line. Coy Hdqs & Platoon in 2" Line with 1 Platoon in retrenchment. They worked all night digging retrenchment which was just dark & considerable amount of sniping all night

May 15 " "

During morning enemy could be seen digging trench at out 70° behind all support N. of Sanctuary. There we enfiled for about 2 hours at ranges of about 25* but finally had to withdraw on account of being trenched. All quiet during day except for 9.02 & of sniping. Enemy artillery seem to have completely stopped. Reinforcements that trench are advancing Sardis. Continued working on retrenchment all day. 9.02 deal of sniping all day practically no shelling fire from enemy who have undoubtedly moved their guns

May 16 " "

Another quiet day. Enemy have Cavalry division visited trenches with a view to relieving us to-morrow.

May 17 " "

Army Form C. 2118.

WAR DIARY
or
INTELLIGENCE SUMMARY.
(Erase heading not required.)

Instructions regarding War Diaries and Intelligence Summaries are contained in F. S. Regs., Part II. and the Staff Manual respectively. Title pages will be prepared in manuscript.

Hour, Date, Place	Summary of Events and Information	Remarks and references to Appendices
SANCTUARY WOOD May 18th	Considerable amount of Sniping during the day. At night relieved in trenches by 19th Hussars and Regt marched back to 2 Bivouacs about 2 miles S.E. of POPERINGHE a distance of 14 miles, left billets at 9 pm and at 9.15 reached T/H 3AM. 4to Platoons of H van left at—SANCTUARY WOOD to remain in Reserve arriving 16, 2 Platoons S.M.D.L.I gathering tools.	Casualties: No 7920 Sgt Cooper D wounded 11734 Cpl Hughes D " 9052 P.E Pratt B D KILLED 11799 Pl Laurance WR KILLED 16262 " WR R/m Lt Langdon 2 Glous R joined 2Lt Poston "
	B.H.Q moved all in bivouacs except 2 Platoons above by 9.15 AM Signal WR R/m none wanting	
19th	Continued in Bivouac. 2 Platoons 4 Coy joined at 7 AM. 4t 12.30pm the Brigade (1st B.S.H) 2 Gordon Highlanders 2 Glou R) were inspected by the C in C Sir John French. No incident.	
20th	Continued in Bivouac. During day fatigues etc and recreation and small parades. Drafts of 135 men & NCOs arrived from England.	
21st		
22nd	Continued in Bivouac. All NCOs were formed at POPERINGHE.	
23rd	" "	
24th	" "	
25	At 5.30 PM received wire from Gen'l 1st B.I. 3rd Corps stated that front of 28th Div was eight of 4th Div and being attacked. Gas being used. Regt will hold your Bn in readiness to move to VLAMERTINGHE at short notice by motor or transport will about to M to At 6.30 AM moved forward "Prepare to" At 9 AM revd order to move to HQS 7th HS at 3.30 pm. Batts answered Rest 9.30 pm HERTSHOEK—REWING HEYST OUDERDOM "	
26th ACTS 9.45 Amch VYRS	Contained with HQs & Regt supplied Esct Staff Warr Offr Mr etc during Moving. Revd Wire.	
" 17	Contained in Huts in Reserve to 28th Div and under orders ready to move at ½ hour notice. At 6 PM revd orders Regt 27th Div would concy with 3rd ARMY Corps Attlumps (Lt Col Sm & Potter R/A D/O) 2nd Army Fd St. Row to ARMENTIERES to convey a 28th Div would if prepared at 4 AM to LOLRE of Everard Run tomorrow Georges & Germans in Garrison to remain in Reserve	Lt D.K. Germain Glou R Capt H.K. Smith 3rd G.R. joined

WAR DIARY
or
INTELLIGENCE SUMMARY.
(Erase heading not required.)

Army Form C. 2118.

Instructions regarding War Diaries and Intelligence Summaries are contained in F.S. Regs., Part II. and the Staff Manual respectively. Title pages will be prepared in manuscript.

Hour, Date, Place	Summary of Events and Information	Remarks and references to Appendices
LOCRE May 28th 1915	At 10 AM relieved by 1 Suffolks. Marched off followed by Company 10-10 AM route VIAHERTON OODERDUM - WESTOUTRE to LOCRE. Bivouac there for night	
Field Sgt 12 mile S of STEENWERCK May 29 '15	Marched out at 5 AM, 10 AM at BAILEUL. Coy officers proceeded to ARMENTIERE by motor-bus to visit trenches to be taken over by us from 16/13. to morrow night. Troops paused to be rested in company Sgt.	
1st Trenches HQ Gnr'ln Sutton May 30 East of CHAPELLE nr CHAPELLE ARMENTIERE	Marched out of bivouacs 1-50 PM (via RAC ST MAUR) bridge W. ARMENTIERE by route of chapelle & had tea. Marched 7-15 PM in CHAPELLE ARMENTIERE. One section of 1st Battn N Lancs 16 Bde 13th Div CHAPELLE ARMENTIERE Relief completed by 11.30 PM. Very quiet night. Trenches used HQ St.	..... ✗
" May 31	1st Trenches. Enemy (19" Saxon Corps) to our front very quiet. Day entry part of wooden Give Fire well seen + narrow ls.	Casualties— A/Cpl 7/2 Price No 5249 x Lce Cpl D.G. Worrell — 1st/ B . . " "

81st Inf.Bde.
27th Div.

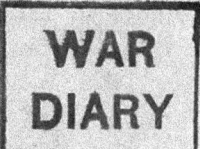

2nd BATTN. THE GLOUCESTERSHIRE REGIMENT.

J U N E

1 9 1 5

2nd Battalion The Gloucestershire Regiment.

June 1915

[In Trenches H.Q. Centre Section near CHAPELLE ARMENTIERES]

June 2	A Little shelling during day. Cotton arm.strong M.Guns fire during night. Another all night in improving trans [transverse] trench.	Casualty No 8797 Pte London (D) KILLED
June 3	Very quiet all day. A Little shelling and M.Gun fire during night.	Nil
June 4th	" " Hd. Qrs moved to dugouts in ORCHARD	
June 5th	Very quiet all day. "It was thought that morning H.Guns which had been firing unadvisedly in enemy's transport at night had been spotted in consequence in future will M.G. & rifle through the loophole is knocked in the wall. Retired team not open fire again that night	Casualty No 6449 Cpl. Carpenter wounded. Nil
June 6th	A Little shelling on both sides. Enemy M.Gs quiet all night. Battn very lightly sniped Trenches improved.	Nil
June 7th	Very quiet all day. Enemy shelled Farm Hackneine in the afternoon causing 98th Battery to with draw & on demolition Pte Nay, who picked Rim on Bois Grenier Gun duel a Snipe Shelling. At night cottages occupied by H.G. got firm from both sides.	All Wounding Cpl Alley

INTELLIGENCE SUMMARY.

(Erase heading not required.)

Instructions regarding War Diaries and Intelligence Summaries are contained in F.S. Regs., Part II. and the Staff Manual respectively. Title pages will be prepared in manuscript.

Hour, Date, Place	Summary of Events and Information	Remarks and references to Appendices
Trenches M&Gn ORCHARD CHAPELLE ARMENTIERES June 8th	Some shelling at Rue des Bois. All quiet in front of us. A Little M Gun fire. 2nd Bn of 6th Worcesters joined today. C&Hand work on 1st support line & 2nd support line & 2 officers of 6th Worcesters joined today.	(ii)
" June 9th	Lieut. Quinton C&Hand went on support line. Major Priest Oxen Regt known (L.G. Col. Unwin) wounded. 30 Connection day.	(ii)
" June 10th	A Little shelling about midday. C&Hand work on support line. 1 Coy 9th R Fusiliers (Kitchener's) sent into trenches for 24 hours for instruction.	
" June 11th		
" June 12th	More shelling. Heavy arrival on our Left wing again tonight. Work on support Trenches Casualty No 9051 Pte Anstrum C Coy (A) wounded. Arty shelling completed. Draft 4 officers 75 men arrived.	
HQ Rue du National ARMENTIERES June 13th	Relieved by 1st A&SH. WH of supports No 11 A.M. Battn went into billets in ARMENTIERE. Strength of Battn 23 officers. HOSPICE. RUE du PATORES. Except A Coy left in Reserve to 1st A SH with 3 Platoons in Subsidiary line. 1 Platoon in 2nd Support Line. Remainder of Battn in Divisional Reserve. 92/ Other Ranks	
" June 14th	Continued in Billets.	
" June 15th	Battn bathed except A Coy. Returned A Coy in Subsidiary line with C Coy. Enemy dropped a few shells into the town about 4pm and again 9pm.	(ii)
" "	C&Hand in billets. Coys doing Grenade Cubs & musketry. All ranks issued with "Smoke helmets"	
" June 16th	Continued in billets. Relieved C Coy - Subsidiary line with B Coy.	do
" June 17th	A&D B Coy took over 67 Trench from Coxon Highlanders. D Coy went into Subsidiary line in Reserve to 1 A.S.H.	
Trench RQ ORCHARD 46 CHAPELLE ARMENTIERES June 18th	Relieved 1 A.S.H. in trenches, relief completed by 10.30pm. Busy quiet.	
" June 19th	Busy 4 A&E firing A day. Snipers: enemy have been very active. LILLE worked bit from numerous grounds.	Casualty. No 18986 Pte Cooper B wounded.
" June 20th	A letter number of shells during the afternoon from both sides. Sounds of many Supports but Heavy Machine fields could here nothing. Lt Col Dennis took over command of Regt. Metropole burg any quite a repeat of own line.	
	A rather number of shelling during the afternoon from both sides. Searchlight again used Metropole. Enemy using searchlight N of LILLE Road. Enemy using	

W. Unwin Capt Ag

INTELLIGENCE SUMMARY.

(Erase heading not required.)

Instructions regarding War Diaries and Intelligence Summaries are contained in F.S. Regs., Part II. and the Staff Manual respectively. Title pages will be prepared in manuscript.

Hour, Date, Place	Summary of Events and Information	Remarks and references to Appendices
Near HQ Gun Trench ORCHARD nr CHAPELLE ARMENTIERES June 21st	Very quiet. Could hear rattling of Enemy's waggons. Enemy still using signal lights at night. Went over engagement by Lyotts in ARMENTIERE. A LINE HQrs for 1 Coy of 9th Buffs attached to the Regt for 48 hours instruction.	Casualties: No 1 No. 161 Shears DCM awarded DCM to gallant work. Making 6 raids. No 261 Shears DCM to gallant in courageous action under heavy fire. Effective strength — Officers 25. Other Ranks 912. Casualties June 20 —
" June 22nd	Enemy shelled Sunken Road Trench 64 about 1 P.M. Very quiet all night.	2 Lt. F. Shell 3rd Essex Attd Wounded
" June 23rd	Lot of movement of Transport heard behind Genin Lie in early morng. Listening Posts of our Genin were slightly away some of then guns & troops. Enemy extraordinary quiet all day. At night patrols could hear Transport moving Practically all night.	Casualties Nil Following appointed to Division by Sir Wm French. — 5th April Lt Col G. S Tulloch. — Capt A C Vincy. — Capt T D Berger. Lt W G Chapman. — Capt G Capman. — Lt Farmar. —
HOSPICE CIVILE ARMENTIERE June 24th	Very quiet all day. About 6 pm Some artillery fire. Rifing completed by 10 pm. Battn relieved by 1 A & S H in ARMENTIERES, less D Coy A nothing 67 Trench and A Coy in Reserve in Subsidiary Line. Good.	Casualties No 1 Following appointed in Gazette For gallantry and distinguished Service in the field — dt of Gaz 3rd Military Cross Capt & Adjutant A C Vincy.
" June 25th	Continued in billets.	Casualties 16299 Pte Trotter. M. (2) wounded (at duty) 19865 — Haggerman P. D — —
" June 26th	"	Millray Capt/Major

Forms/C. 2118/10.

Army Form C. 2118.

WAR DIARY
or
INTELLIGENCE SUMMARY.
(Erase heading not required).

Instructions regarding War Diaries and Intelligence Summaries are contained in F.S. Regs., Part II. and the Staff Manual respectively. Title pages will be prepared in manuscript.

Hour, Date, Place.	Summary of Events and Information.	Remarks and references to Appendices.
RIDGE WOOD ARMENTIÈRES June 24th	D Coy in Trench 67 had been bombarded with hand grenades about midday. Otherwise a quiet day. Tout sur vers Tanche. C Coy to T 63. B returned to Pearson Billiards.	Casualty :— No 6352 Pte Worthy D Coy KILLED by hand grenade. Armentières. Funeral of R.I.H. Officers 26. Other Ranks. 905
June 25th	A & D Coy returned to E.R.A. Hospice Civil. C Coy returned to trench 63 & B Coy remained in Reserve to A & D in Subsidiary lines.	Casualty No 7031 Cpl Evans to C Coy Wounded
June 29th	Continued in E.R.A.	Casualty Nil
Hd Qrs to Touquet June 30th RUE DES BOIS	Relieved 1 A & S H in Trenches 60 61 62 63 (Rue du Bois) 1 Coy in each. Relief completed by 11 PM. Very quiet during night.	Casualty Nil

81st Inf.Bde.
27th Div.

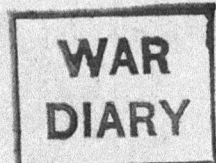

2nd BATTN. THE GLOUCESTERSHIRE REGIMENT.

J U L Y

1 9 1 5

2nd Battalion The Gloucestershire Regiment.

July 1915

Date			Casualties
July 1st	[Hd Qrs & Trenches RUE DU BOIS]	Day quiet up to 6 PM when there was a little artillery fire. Enemy fire 1 or 2 Snipers all quiet during the night.	Nil
July 2nd	"	Quiet all the morning. 2 Enemy aircraft overhead about 6 pm. Enemy 2" gun + a few HE shells at 6.30 pm lobbed at Tunnel + near Bn HQ. Very heavy artillery fire from East.	Nil
July 3rd	"	Quiet all day. Considerable amount of HE & shrapnel between 9pm+11 pm. Considerable amount of sniping from both sides all night. Enemy's patrols busy again to-night. Very heavy artillery fire from W & E	Nil
July 4th	"	Enemy working hard on their trenches, day + night. Considerable amount of sniping from both sides. Very quiet night. Heavy artillery fire from W+E	Nil
July 5th	"	Enemy again very quiet. A day's still very busy working on their trenches. During July 3 days our sniper's claim to have hit 12 enemy including 2 officers. Enemy shelled Trench X. without any result. A French aircraft was brought down by shell fire in the afternoon. Many attempts to stop our aircraft were made but in vain.	Casualties:— No 11309 Pte G Mortem. C. Coy. KILLED buried CHAPELLE D'ARMENTIERS. No 1906 Pte Maunder to hospital wounded. All Wing Corp:— [signature]
July 6th	"	Enemy aircraft very active. At 11.55 AM our Arty, opened fire on our guns. Shots fell into ARMENTIERES. They kept up anything from W to E. Their shells from 4.50 PM being short. Enemy patrols to the South into ARMENTIERES. They kept up anything but haul under. 80 PH being started moving for T. 61 being unknown. In fact our guns all quiet by 9 pm. Returned by 1.AM.SH Paths returned to

Army Form C. 2118.

WAR DIARY
or
INTELLIGENCE SUMMARY.
(Erase heading not required.)

Instructions regarding War Diaries and Intelligence
Summaries are contained in F. S. Regs., Part II.
and the Staff Manual respectively. Title pages
will be prepared in manuscript.

Hour, Date, Place	Summary of Events and Information	Remarks and references to Appendices
HOSPICE CIVIL ARMENTIERES July 6th	Moved to H.M.A Hospice civil ARMENTIERES. A Coy removed a Stationary Line in Reserve to 1 A. & S. H.	Casualties:— No 3086 Pte Chatwin A.R. A Coy KILLED No 497 " Baxter T. A " KILLED No 19691 " Crackley W. B. " wounded No 8382 L/Cpl Keegan H. B. " " No 9402 Cpl. Tallboy A.D. B. " " No 1021.1 Pte Fisher W. A. " " No 7093 Pte Painter B. " "
" July 7th	Continued in billets.	Casualties Nil
" July 8th	Continued in billets.	Nil
" July 9th	B Coy relieved A Coy as Reserve to 1 A. & S. H. in billets.	Nil 8625 L/Cpl Margetts D Coy wounded
" July 10th	Continued in billets	Nil
" July 11th	Buffs paraded for C.E. 11.30 A.M. Entertained in billets. Enemy dropped a few shells and went into ARMENTIERES. (S.L.I.) into billets but no damage.	8625 L.C. Margetts Ref.No. 11.30 am buried ERQUINGHEM-LYS.
H.Qr. Trenches RUE du BOIS July 12th	Relieved 1 A.&S.H. in trenches 60. 61. 62. 63. Relief completed by 10.30pm. From information in front of 60 enemy still on defensive. They have practically completed trench in front of their entanglement and filled it with cows. Quiet to our front during the night.	Casualties Nil
" July 13th	Some heavy rifle fire about 1½ mi/m to own left about 2 A.M. A little sharp shooting during the day on both sides. Enemy's aircraft fairly active. From reconnaissance made enemy have dug a Trench 15 to 20 wide apparently 4 feet deep and as given in front of their parapets. 2 M.Gs trench they two poles hoisted over and they are now standing in stacks. About 11pm sent them some offensive fire at down their two [illegible] of our Trenches. Showed soon them enemy their line is weakly held. About 9pm heavy rifle fire heard from direction of PLUGSTREET, lasted about 25 min. Fired a fair enquiry all night.	Casualty: No. 19935 Pte Neat B Coy wounded M Waring Capt/A A. R Glover 2 Glover

(73989) W4141—463. 400,000. 9/14. H.&J.Ltd. Forms/C. 2118/10.

Army Form C. 2118.

WAR DIARY
or
INTELLIGENCE SUMMARY.
(Erase heading not required).

Instructions regarding War Diaries and Intelligence Summaries are contained in F.S. Regs., Part II. and the Staff Manual respectively. Title pages will be prepared in manuscript.

Hour, Date, Place.	Summary of Events and Information.	Remarks and references to Appendices.
Hd Qrs Tranchée Rue du Bois, July 14th Station	In front of T.60 enemy sniped freely actively up to daylight. Enemy still working on other in front of Rein parapet. Seen anything fire during the day. Enemy's concentration in the morning. Our Heavy [Artillery] firing hard during afternoon from S.E. Heavy rain during night, consequently very little firing. Enemy shell ARMENTIÈRES pretty heavily during the day.	Casualties NIL.
July 15th	Enemy have at last spotted our Sapen lop.60.6 to ESTAMINET Rue du Bois and attempted to have it be abandoned. About 8AM many shrapnel over 5 rifle grenades into T.61 2Sgts to damage done. Very little firing during the day. Our snipers very active, between 6pm & 7-3.30pm. Enemy much active sniping on both sides. Enemy the machine gun very busy firing on men working in their saps & trenches so that many are from to their Sapheads in front of 62 Front. Enemy snipers active from 3AM to 7AM. Act [indecipherable] at 6-10 PM very heavy [indecipherable] into T.61 and Richards St. No damage. Our snipers tried Trent Houston firing 36 Rounds and rifle grenades and 123BRFA fired 6 rounds. This stopped the enemy the rest of the day. Enemy 5th busy on their [indecipherable] St. busy all night.	Casualties NIL. NIL
July 16th		
July 17th	Except for fairly active Sniper shots from enemy 9 AM- 5pm quiet day. About 4pm enemy seemed between our [indecipherable] & Richard's Ft & ARMENTIÈRES and we do have no [indecipherable] up on front. 9 AM 54 wounded A Coy in T.63 by snipe of a fighter. Another. Enemy's sniper killed 1 Master in Richard's Ft Trench during 1st ASB Coy on Schobury Line. [indecipherable] T.61. Enemy [indecipherable] night. Party move 5 W. Army. Hope Snr, 6.7 HKs OD DSO commanding 29 Div. [indecipherable] 3.30 [indecipherable] from trench	NIL dWinny

Army Form C. 2118.

WAR DIARY
or
INTELLIGENCE SUMMARY.
(Erase heading not required).

Instructions regarding War Diaries and Intelligence Summaries are contained in F.S. Regs., Part II. and the Staff Manual respectively. Title pages will be prepared in manuscript.

Hour, Date, Place.	Summary of Events and Information.	Remarks and references to Appendices.
RUE de FAUBOURG de LILLE July 18th ARMENTIERES	A certain amount of shelling fire from both sides during the day. Enemy sniping pretty keen all day. In the afternoon 2 woman & child were seen behind the German lines. Relieved by 1 A&S H. Relief completed by 10·30 PM and Batt'n returned to billets ARMENTIERES.	Casualty No 5893 Pte Brooks D Coy KILLED. buried CH. ARMENTIERES No 13873 Pte Tanner B Coy Wounded. Strength of Batt'n. Officers 26 Other Ranks 936 Casualty N.1.
July 19th	Continued in billets. Enemy's aircraft very active in early morning and evening.	Casualty N.1.
July 20th	Enemy's aircraft again active. Owing to ¼ A&S.H taking over another Trench (59) on the right of ARMENTIERE LA HOUSSOYE RAILWAY, D Coy went into Subsidiary Line in Reserve.	N.1
July 21st	About 5·30 AM enemy shelled the Town, a few 4·2's but mostly Pipsqueaks. Draft arrived from England 1 officer (2nd Lt Tanner) 520 other Ranks. moral very young sober, but on the whole good.	N.1
July 22nd	Continued in billets. Enemy shelled Town about 5·30 PM putting 1 Pipsqueak into Batt. H Q. no damage done. Half of shells burst near ASYLUM.	Strength Officers 26 Other Ranks 975.
23	Our artillery active about 4-15 p.m. C Coy returned D in Subsidiary Line.	N.1.
July 24th	Our artillery active practically all day. Enemy in far as we were concerned very quiet.	
July 25th	Relieved 1 A&S.H in Trenches 59, 60, 61, 62. Relief completed by 10·30pm Up to midnight except for usual Sniping very quiet. Down further own aircraft fairly active.	Casualties. —
In Trenches H Coy RUE d. BOIS SECTION July 26th	An quiet during the morning. At 2pm enemy started shelling BOIS GRENIER LINE from DESPERIQUES to HOUPLINES. My burst a haystack and dropped 6 shells in end of HAYSTACK AVENUE. They kept up the bombardt. till 3·30pm and although they hit the parapet often there was no casualty. From 6pm to 7·30 enemy's and our artillery were very active, our heavy 2·10 star hit a captive from 6pm. Our artillery fired a good 60 shells at clay pigeon and considerable explosion against the Enemy's trench. Our fire during the night was carried out 40 rpr pm against the Enemy's front steadily by 5 minutes rapid.	No 5312 Cpl Bashy B Coy Wounded. A.W.

WAR DIARY or INTELLIGENCE SUMMARY

Army Form C. 2118.

Hour, Date, Place.	Summary of Events and Information.	Remarks and references to Appendices.
Trenches N¼ Coy RUE du BOIS Sector July 27ᵗʰ	Artillery fire mostly from our guns, all day. About 4 pm then received MG gun shelling T.6.1.6.2. GRAND HARAS FARM road, LA VALLEE and RUE MARQUART. Enemy replied by shelling ARMENTIERES and West of HAYSTACK AVENUE. Any 8 pm our guns fire had ceased. During day continued sniping. Enemy with any any on their trenches. About 4 AM enemy aircraft observed flying low by our guns. Our aircraft in action from 5:30 pm to 8 pm. At night enemy kept opening with short bursts of rapid rifle & MG fire. When enemy working parties were seen during the night which were continuously sniped by. Our patrol out from 11:30. Spotted and working party which we got MG on to. Still safe good works.	Casualty 2. Lieut K.J.B. Mann (attached) 3ʳᵈ Divs wounded
" July 28ᵗʰ	Enemy fired a good many shells into ARMENTIERES and our battery during the day and also put a few Shrapnel about midday behind and into 59 and 60 Trenches. Our guns were busy all day on enemy's parapet, LA VALLEE and known behind their lines. A quiet night.	Casualties:- No 9895 Pte Bentz B Coy. Wounded. No 14476 1 Cpl Hampton B Coy "
" July 29ᵗʰ	Have not heard fire them much from both sides. Enemy shelled BOIS GRENIER LINE, HAYSTACK AVENUE and behind T.59.T.60 but no damage done. About 10 AM enemy put a good many shells into CHAPELLE ARMENTIERES. From 9 pm to midnight there was a good deal of rifle fire for our front also on our right. A first an unusually many night. Enemy occasionally fired Salvos at LEVEL CROSSING near FERM DESPLANQUES. He opened by shelling Rue Sulens opposite 60 which always had the effect of stopping him temporarily. During the night we got up another left French Mortar to our salient at RUE du BOIS we now have 1 Aostillian Trench Mortar firing 35 lb bombs and a heavy Trench Mortar firing 4 lb bombs	Casualty 17269 Pte Cleveland C. Coy Wounded.

[signature]

Army Form C. 2118.

WAR DIARY
or
INTELLIGENCE SUMMARY.
(Erase heading not required).

Hour, Date, Place.	Summary of Events and Information.	Remarks and references to Appendices.

Trenches RUE du BOIS Section
July 30. 15.

About 1.30 AM heavy firing heard from PLOEGSTREET direction and rapid fire and bombing about 1 mile on our right lasting for about 20 mins.

The following Operation Orders issued:-
1. It has been decided that to commemorate 415 AM Drum Chg. 29th GLOUCESTERS PROTrenches opposite our trenches 59, 60, 61, 62 from H. Parka Place 31 July 1915 with the object of :-
(a) Killing Germans. (b) Capturing enemy's parapet and win an opportunity for an attack. (c) Ascertaining the movement of our troops in case of a bombardment by our artillery.
2. To this end the following programme will be carried out:-
(a) During the day our Artillery will register and the town and destroy hostile parapet.
(b) 6.45 pm to 6.50 pm Artillery will intensify.
(c) 6.50 pm to 6.57 pm Artillery bombard the parapets in the above Trenches with our burst of shrapnel and HE Grainf fire, with the object of smashing the parapet. Heavy concentration will be the object of shells. The intensity to slacken in any salient. There will be no concentration. Our Troops on grounds occupying to advancing & to shatter shelter of surprise on enemy front line, and her parapets, where his mpmnts arms.
(d) 7 pm our artillery bombardment of enemy's Trenches will commence. Prior to this heavy infantry will be withdrawn from parapet and will exactly shell Trenches and dugouts to minimum of loss (a) men to carry flares (b) bags will be packed in the Fire Trench on both sides.
(e) 10 PM our Artillery will search the enemy's Trenches. Infantry will return in (a) above.
3. In order to deceive the enemy on the night 30/31, Communication of the Trenches 60-61 will march with external slithering attack slithering the party would attempt attack of after Trenches was contemplated. Three shelters stalked where the plan so as to be visible from the German Trenches.
4. Coy Commanders will take steps at once to ensure that a quantity of filled sandbags on at hand at various points along their Trenches, with which to repair any damage that may be done to their parapets.
5. At 4 pm 31 July 1915 all watches will be synchronized from being passed to Artillery and Company Commds from H.Q. 2nd Gloucester Regt.
6. The Reserve Coy (C & S Highlanders) has 1 Platoon will move via RAILWAY AVENUE into the Bde H.Q Q lines a Glos R at 5pm 31 July 1915.
7. Reports to Batt H.Q HQ August.

30th July 1915

A.C. Vicary Captain
Adjutant 2nd Batt. Gloucestershire Regt.

[struck through] The 9th Royal Scots being T.62 on our left arrived on relief in 15 9pm with bunch of reports on enemy's "Salient" at 6-4.30 P.M. to 6-57 P.M. artillery attacked.
Copies of above by Lt. Col. W.B. Emery CMG Regt for artillery attached.
During the day Company dug a few Battling Trenches at 7.60, 61 and at Batt H.Q. Our enemy action from officers of enemy shot at a few Emplacements H. Guards. Open shot into the a few aft will on off-sh Emdnt. Be attend.
8 pm to 9 pm during the night [struck through]

A.W. [signature]

WAR DIARY or INTELLIGENCE SUMMARY

Army Form C. 2118.

Hour, Date, Place.	Summary of Events and Information.	Remarks and references to Appendices.
Trenches RUE du BOIS Sector H.Q. 3/4acy	Enemy attempt any action about 6 A.M. Our aeroplanes shelled without effect. During morning our Artillery syncing on enemy's trenches opposite sq. 59. 60. 61. 62. 63 64 and enemy's communication and reserve trenches. This caused enemy to reply by shelling at intervals our trenches, and BOIS GRENIER LINE between HAYSTACK AVENUE and DESPLANQUES FARM. At 5 P.M Our Artillery started shelling enemy's wire to enemy communication Trench 61 and 60 and SL Mld A Coy. Support Trenches, CHAPELLE ARMENTIERES and BOIS GRENIER LINE At 6.30 P.M Our and Hun Artillery were busy active. At 6.45 PM 2 Coy Hun was sent up from our Hd Qrs. Our Artillery immediately caused Huns and our Infantry opened rifle bursts of rapid fire and M.Gun fire. Enemy kept shelling our trenches and BOIS GRENIER LINE especially near DESPLANQUES FARM when 2 guns of 98th Battery had pointed up to our standing kept up their fire until 6-57 pm when they ceased and withdrew to Artillery shelter trenches behind the parapet. Enemy immediately opened with rapid rifle fire, evidently expecting an attack. At 7PM we opened fire with our 2 half Trench Mortars and Artillery Trench Mortars throwing a 35-16 bombs, each of these got off 25 rounds. At H. Some tons our guns bombarded Hun trenches M. 4.7.5 bombarding Hun parapet and wire on immediate rear and over Field guns bursting shrapnel on Hun parapet. Enemy in up to sq. H4 and 98th Batty was front DESPLANQUES and BOIS GRENIER LINE to South side of RAILWAY LINE and behind T.59. Enemy apparently only had 2 Field Batteries and 1 Howitzer Battery, kept Reply against these very weakly. This only lasted 260 yds in sq. H of T60 Jaw so many shells over parapet their Support to our RAILWAY line mobility was a Coup Houses built up from our Hd Qrs. Our Artillery immediately stopped rapid fire. At 7.15 Enemy who said down and by 7.30 PM they had ceased. Our Artillery continued to their Salvoes he wanted no casualties and no damage done close to our parapet. There was considerable damage done to enemy's parapet and their Sap opposite T.59 was very badly damaged. At 1-10 PM our guns again bombarded their trenches. Enemy replied by firing a few S.W.B. into ARMENTIERES road, opening up rifle fire and sending up numerous flares and throwing up 3 Searchlights. Our M.Guns opened fire on the Hostile flare Searchlights made 2 efforts to keep going but finally expired. At 10.45 PM situation normal except for considerable amount of wild firing from the enemy. By midnight every thing was practically quiet.	Casualties N.1
1 August	Enemy kept quiet all day. Rations, Rations Rum and S.PM carrying fatigues into our line Incident to our left about BOIS G RETHERTS. Enemy any casualties this camp and when opened Rumours. No. 8978 Pte Elliott A. D Coy killed Machine. Several kinds of work for a tour left.	wounded

J. Whiley

81st Inf.Bde.
27th Div.

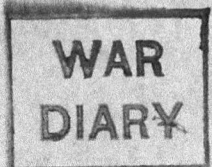

2nd BATTN. THE GLOUCESTERSHIRE REGIMENT.

A U G U S T

1 9 1 5

WAR DIARY
or
INTELLIGENCE SUMMARY.
(Erase heading not required).

Army Form C. 2118.

Instructions regarding War Diaries and Intelligence Summaries are contained in F.S. Regs, Part II. and the Staff Manual respectively. Title pages will be prepared in manuscript.

Hour, Date, Place.	Summary of Events and Information.	Remarks and references to Appendices.
Aug 2nd	At 3 AM enemy manned Trench 60 and also Moore first lines rifle grenades over. We replied heavy firing 10.35 lb bombs from Artillery Trench Howitzer about 25" bombs from heavy Trench Mortar about 20 rifles grenades. At same time 152 Bty & A.S.3 Howr Bty shelled enemy's salient opposite T.60. Their fire completely silenced the enemy and at 4 AM everything was quiet. At 7-45 AM enemy biplane appeared returning to German lines from direction of ARMENTIÈRES. It was shelled by our anti-aircraft and it seems to 10th Batt. Apparently in the engine as her engine stopped and a long stream of smoke came from... She dropped very quickly and came down heavily about 1 mile behind enemy's lines. Little artillery fire about the day otherwise quiet.	Casualty No 19448 Pte Rogers B Coy accidentally wounded.
HQ L'HALLOBEAU near ERQUINGHEM. Aug 3rd	11 PM the Battalion marched to bivouac at TRS L'HALLOBEAU relieved by 1st KSLI completed by 3 AM. Bivouac at ERQUINGHEM near LYS. A.A.	
" Aug 4th	Bath, bivouac and billets in Farms in vicinity of L'HALLOBEAU. All Coys training, drill etc. & riflemen football contest &c	
" Aug 5th	Ditto. Draft of 20 other Ranks arrived from England.	
" Aug 6th	"	
" Aug 7th	" & afternoon B.D.C. Coys led Coy sports & evening Regimental Concert carried	
" Aug 8th	by Divl. Band.	
" Aug 9th	Church Parade.	
" Aug 10th	Very heavy Artillery fire from 2 AM to 4 AM lined up Road & looked say over VOORMEZEELE. Started marching on Support line near BOIS GRENIER. 60 mm by day, 150 by night. The heavy firing lasted from 2 AM to 4 AM proved to be 16th & 18th Bdes attacking at HOOGE. They succeeded in taking 1500 yds of German Trench & 3 officers 150 other ranks prisoners and making one hot down trench. & killed by 5 IM fire. Very heavy into YPRES. Twenty to lot Brit took over command new Hot Down trench.	Strength of Battn. Officers 27 Other Ranks 992
" Aug 11th	Continued work on BOIS GRENIER line.	A. Wisong Capt Adjt

Army Form C. 2118.

WAR DIARY
or
INTELLIGENCE SUMMARY.
(Erase heading not required).

Instructions regarding War Diaries and Intelligence Summaries are contained in F.S. Regs., Part II. and the Staff Manual respectively. Title pages will be prepared in manuscript.

Hour, Date, Place.	Summary of Events and Information.	Remarks and references to Appendices.
H.Q. L'HALLO BEAU Aug 12th	Continued work at BOIS GRENIER. Army Cmdr (Sir Douglas Haig) visited H.Q. Gen.	Strength—
" " Aug 13th	"	Officers 27 Other Ranks 999
" " Aug 14th	Draft of 20 Other Ranks arrived from England	
" " Aug 15th	Regimental Concert visited by Div. Band	
	Stopped work on BOIS GRENIER. Following orders issued. 87.1B will relieve 82.1B in Trenches 50–66 Monday 16th inst. 1 A & S H will relieve 1 Leins in night Subs in T.50.57.52.53. 1 Coy ⓑ 2 Glous R will relieve 1 Coy DCLI, as Reserve to 1 A & S H, in BOIS GRENIER LINE from ROAD JUNCTION H.30.b. to RIVIERE des LAIES Two of relief for B Coy will be notified later. The Battn in order of march, Sigs: Sapps: Grenadier Coy: — B. D. C. A. M. G. — S.Bs. will be formed up in Column of route, head of Column to be at head in point H.1.b.96 ready to march off 3:15 PM. 16th inst, Route ERQUINHEM BRIDGE to B.1.b.6 RUE DELETTRE. Battns will do their own tool arrangements with farms.	
H.Q. Farm RUE DELETTRE Aug 16th	Reported by to Corps Commander Lt. Gen. W.P. Pulteney KCB DSO at 10 AM., who inspected the coy afterwards with this approval. Marched off from billets 3:15 PM 16 billets in RUE DELETTRE. Arrived 5:15 PM. B Coy took up position in BOIS GRENIER on Reserve to 1 A&S.L.14 at 9:30 PM	
" " Aug 17th	At 5 PM received orders to relieve own Trenches 48–49. 30 PM Ash: 6–2 morrow night. A Coy relieved 2nd Northlands in 74.B. B Coy 2 Northlands in 74.9A. C Coy 1. A&S.H. in T.S.D. D Coy in BOIS GRENIER LINE as Reserve. Relief completed by 10 PM. Trenches have been hotly left up left of work against. Very little storm. Continual sniping all night otherwise quiet.	18/8/16 Coy have spared from hospital Casualty No. 15874 Pte Wiggings B Coy No 8793 Pte Burnett B Coy Wounded
In Trenches HQ I.31.a.6.7 Aug 19th	Continued sniping by the enemy who sniper from behind their lines. Continued work on Communication Trench & Fire Trenches. Enemy first 5–9" Houtzers shells 300 W of BOIS GRENIER otherwise no shelling. Staff	Strength— Officers 27 Other Ranks 962. No 8373 Pte Betteridges A Coy Wounded No 19235 Pte Brunt B Coy Wounded

A.W. ___

Army Form C. 2118.

WAR DIARY
or
INTELLIGENCE SUMMARY.
(Erase heading not required).

Instructions regarding War Diaries and Intelligence Summaries are contained in F.S. Regs., Part II. and the Staff Manual respectively. Title pages will be prepared in manuscript.

Hour, Date, Place.	Summary of Events and Information.	Remarks and references to Appendices.
HQ Trenches I 31 a 4 7 Aug 20th	Enemy's snipers busy all day. Trench behind Germans has will HQ. The hut the effect of quietening enemy's snipers. Good deal of firing during the night from both sides. Snipers Enemy's aircraft seen active from 8 AM to 7 PM.	Casualties No 9085 L/Cpl Hall B Coy KILLED No 85247 Sergt Engt A Coy wounded No 16186 Pte Gardiner B Coy wounded
" Aug 21st	Continued work all night and day as before during the day. At night enemy's snipers sticking down. A very quiet night.	Casualty No 10207 Pte Greenhalgh A Coy wounded
" Aug 22nd	Continued work as yesterday. Beginning to see some result for the work. Enemy's aircraft very unsteady this morning. Our aircraft chasing any hostile for 5/m. enemy let on one of our by-planes and brought it down on their lines. About 7 pm enemy put a few shells at our new communication trenches. They were soon stopped by 67th Bde RFA shelling enemy's trenches opposite T 48. Fairly quiet night.	Casualty No 17384 Pte Black B Coy Wounded
" Aug 23rd	8 replying to our Trench Howitzer register on Enemy's Trenches (about 50 yds) opposite T 49 enemy shelled HQ and new dugouts on our trenches for an up. apparently. At 9.15pm enemy again shelled snipers' dugouts and our snipers near the upperland & new the Bessing Station, one sub caught 4 probable. LRIE Du BOIS GRENIER road near the Bessing Station, one sub caught 1 PBron HQ Coy tried up to relieve A Coy in T 48 and wounded 4 men. A Coy brought back to LRIE in RUE DU BOIS. T 49, where for the last 2 nights have inspected a mine, during the day night hand digging under floor this Trench in 3 different places.	Casualties No 7494 L/Cpl Thomas Grenadier Coy wounded No 9662 Pte Tingle LH Died Hospital KILLED No 14255 Pte Chinley B Coy D No 20304 " Burnett D No 3119 " Watkins D
" Aug 24th	Enemy quiet during day but very active at night. Keeping hand in support of Coms us in T 49 but do not consider it serious. Flares hand in T 49 but do not consider it serious. Truckers at night.	Casualties No 20573 Pte Saunders B Coy wounded No 3147 Pte Whitter A " " No 1937 Pte Jones A " "
" Aug 25th	Front as before still continued. day & night. German's also breaking hand in Trench 30 x 49 - Reply. Front has Enemy's snipers still active especially during night. Sort stuff No T 49 to be dealt with. Both sides aircraft busy. One hon Commander fired at	Casualty No 9713 Pte Brown B Coy KILLED No Bgr GARNIER
" Aug 26th	Same but firing on left side. Good of supper from enemy. A quiet night but continuous Fishmongers annoyed by the CZAR of RUSSIA opposite 5 poor Prussia Pte Grey 3rd Coy. - 7567 Pte G 99 - 11339 L/Cpl Woodward 6767 CQMS Sheppey 4th Ches. - 16324 Pte 98 Hardage	No 979 Pte Tracey C Coy KILLED Wound Pass GRENIER

Lieut Lathbury Lt-Col adjut

WAR DIARY or INTELLIGENCE SUMMARY

Army Form C. 2118.

(Erase heading not required).

Hour, Date, Place.	Summary of Events and Information.	Remarks and references to Appendices.
In Trenches H.Q. Aug 27th LE BRIDOUX SALIENT I.31.a.8.4 SECTION	Enemy trench guns & air snipers were more active in the 24 hrs. Work still continuing on Major enemy trench. Defences more new long strong out well constructed & gives good concentration trenches. R.E. have extended behind T.40 "Grotesque" & T.43 "Fer Zigzag" & B Co. fatigue parties acting along & in front of this. Enemy S.N. bivvy on the R. front L.I. Enemy snipers very active & hostile artillery & machine gun active all day. Heavy art. firing from Cord S all day.	Strength Officers app. 26. Other Ranks 976. Casualties: No 9330 L.Cpl. Read D Coy wounded. No 15872 Pte. Hurley C. " wounded.
" Aug 28th	S.N. working on defence improvements & trenches up. Breastwork work. Aircraft left actn buzzy. Casualty guns & right fairly active to m.g. night.	Casualties Nil
" Aug 29th	Practically parados work on defences. Fairly good in & days. Started building new barriers in both GRENIER ROAD Tks in morning as evening at night there & field arty on R. shown tkn most and enemy. Rly. from a M.G. on Commanders Hse. night.	Casualty: No 9536 Pte. Pitt. D Coy KILLED buried Bois GRENIER
" Aug 30th	Enemy very busy working on their 2nd line. Enemy fairly quiet. Our aircraft active. Scout fr. 5pm.	Casualties Nil
" Aug 31st	Our heavy & Field guns registering on enemy's trenches & parapet opposite our trenches & Wire, rply. from enemy's Field guns. Trench Molors his our new emplacement and laydn. opposite of totalling a B.G. wall. trenches for trench mortar. The I.T. is extremely ready to attack from her and do our own right. Received other R.O. 23rd B.M. wuekd orders in T.46.49 v 2nd Common in TSO empty. No. 1.2 Sept. The R.O. returning to Lille near ERQUINGHEM. At 5.30 PM men explosion billet & new rgt. speltword by enemy shelling. Later wounded and from 9.9.P.M. met wire. employed more water fatigues & trenches N.10.C.5. at 11.30 PM. & and enemy new shelling crater. Men then used M/R fire & H.G. fire heard always during the nt.	Nil
LA ROLANDERIE Sep 1st FARM in ERQUINGHEM.	Coy morning from reconnaissance in front of T.45 & German had been pushed up. Returned in T.50. Inng. of "Common" at T.45 - 6.9 by & laisder. B Coy bivouaced in Bois GRENIER. Remainder returned to LILLE LA ROLANDERIE FARM in by I AM. 2 sect Cyr was in B.G. Reserve.	Nil Strength Officers 26. O.R. 963

Law B. Lauchlan Lt. Col 6/LIR

81st Inf.Bde.
27th Div.

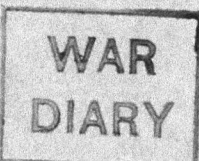

2nd BATTALION THE GLOUCESTERSHIRE REGIMENT.

S E P T E M B E R

1 9 1 5

WAR DIARY
or
INTELLIGENCE SUMMARY.
(Erase heading not required).

Army Form C. 2118.

Instructions regarding War Diaries and Intelligence Summaries are contained in F.S. Regs., Part II. and the Staff Manual respectively. Title pages will be prepared in manuscript.

Hour, Date, Place.		Summary of Events and Information.	Remarks and references to Appendices.
LA ROUANDERIE FARM	Sept 2nd	Continued in Billets	Casualties Nil
"	Sept 3rd	Continued in Billets	Nil Strength 29 officers O.R. 956
"	Sept 4th	Continued in Billets. 2/Lt C.E Wilcombe joined the regiment. Inspection of all clothing equipment + ammunition by H.T.O. A coy relieved B coy in BOIS GRENIER.	Nil
"	Sept 5th	L.B.Mts. Draft 60 men arrived from 4th entrenching battalion	Nil casualties
"	Sept 6th	Continued in Billets.	Nil
"	Sept 7th	Transport, Machine gunners and Grenade coy, strumed off the coy strength from today and Placed under their respective officers for pay, discipline clothing etc.	Casualties 4422 No 6357 Pte Ryan D Coy wounded
"	Sept 8th	Continued in Billets. Experiments carried out by M.G. officers to test efficiency of "D" type S.A.A. in rapid fire Results with M6 satisfactory. M.G. Rifle cannot jamb. D coy relieved A coy at BOIS GRENIER Contained in Billets	Nil
"	Sept 9th	Continued in Billets. 11th West Yorks arrive, attached for instruction.	Nil
"	Sept 10th	Continued in Billets. Lectures given to officers, senior CoSgts N/CpLs of 11th West Yorks. D coy relieved by C coy at BOIS GRENIER.	Nil Strength 28 off & 7 O.R. 999
Sept 11th Sept 12th Sept 13th		Continued in Billets. 10 West Riding arrive, attached for instruction. Heavy artillery fire about 8 AM Enemy shell 4 salvos Bois GRENIER. About 7 AM rumour that our BARGUKEMENT shelled a British plane bringing down German plane near STEINWERK shrapnel amount of activity his during the day.	Casualties No 17234 Pte Ren D Coy KILLED buried at STEINWERK
"	Sep 14	Continued in LBillets. Received orders to march out to manouvres. Approximately at 2.P. 2.7.P.M. moving 69 & 10 strong 8 113.	A Wilson Capt Adj

WAR DIARY
or
INTELLIGENCE SUMMARY.
(Erase heading not required).

Army Form C. 2118.

Instructions regarding War Diaries and Intelligence Summaries are contained in F.S. Regs., Part II. and the Staff Manual respectively. Title pages will be prepared in manuscript.

Hour, Date, Place.	Summary of Events and Information.	Remarks and references to Appendices.
At LA HULLOBEAU nr STEENWERK Sep 15th	Batt marched out of LA BOUDERIE 4 pm arrived in billets near 5-30 PM. Boy in Bois GRENIER LINE. Wounded by 25/1B arrived in billets line 10-30 PM under fire.	Strength: Officers 26. O Ranks 995. Major J Forme posted to England to billets gone command 9th Batt Gloucester Regt.
" Sept 16th	All Batts billeted at ERQUINHEM.	
HQ CAUDESCURE Sep 17th	Batt marched out of billets 6-20 AM. Route STEENWERK - LE VERIER - BLEU - VERTE RUE to billets CAUDESCURE a distance of 10 miles. Batt'n arr in billets 9-30 AM	Sick 3
" "	Visited by G.O.C. 3rd Corps (Lt Gen Sir W P Pulteney KCB, DSO) Reg'ts present on parade. 1st R. Scots - 2 Gloucesters - 2 Cameron Highlanders. 4th A+S.H. 9th Royal Scots. Sir William Pulteney expressed his appreciation of the excellent work done by the Brigade and wished them friendship + goodwill.	Sick 17
From HAZEBROUCK Sep 18th	Church Parade 10 AM. Rumour return to entrain at HAZEBROUCK 9-30 PM. Batt had Plat'n 3 Coy marched off from L.Rd. H AM. Arrived at HAZEBROUCK 1-30 AM and proved to entrain Batt'n and attached by 3 45 AM 2 Platoon D followed by 6 AM. Train nr R 8/18 Kept billets perfect.	Strength: Officers 25. O Ranks 960. Sick 4
HQ WARFUSEE ABANCOURT Sep 20th	Train arrived ABBEVILLE 10 AM for 2 hrs halt Got cost to to man Train arrived GUILLAUCOURT at 1-30 PM (Via AMIENS) Started to detrain here of 2-30 PM. All off and B'trs and Transport on road to WARFUSEE ABANCOURT 3-5 PM Arrived here 4-30 PM and bivouac'd in field SE of village for the night. No casualties during journey. Country very open with few villages widely scattered. Open rolling country L.A.G. comfortable night.	
" Sept 21st	2 Platoon D Coy joined of 1 AM. Remained + L.A.G. Transport moved to park CERISY.	Sick 4
HQ MORCOURT on R. SOMME. Sep 22nd	At 3-30 PM Batt marched out of WARFUSEE ABANCOURT to billets in MORCOURT on the R. SOMME arrived AM in billets by 6 pm	

A Wiseny LtCol
CR

WAR DIARY
or
INTELLIGENCE SUMMARY.
(Erase heading not required).

Instructions regarding War Diaries and Intelligence Summaries are contained in F.S. Regs., Part II. and the Staff Manual respectively. Title pages will be prepared in manuscript.

Hour, Date, Place.		Summary of Events and Information.	Remarks and references to Appendices.
HQ MORCOURT	Sept 23rd	Remained in LHK line. Coys training, physical, close and gun notice drill. 81. 1B now in XIV Corps. 3rd Army.	
"	Sept 24th	Weather fine & warm. Coys training.	
"	Sept 25th	Heavy rain all day. At 9.30pm received news that 1st Army attack had been successful and still progressing, also that the French in CHAMPAGNE had taken whole of German front line and at one point their second German line. Draft of 16 other ranks joined. 31 men sent to RE for Mining. 1 officer 36 OR to XII Corps HQ. to XIV Corps HQ. ft The latter were unfit. Church Parade cancelled in billets.	Strength. Officers 26. O.R. 963
"	Sept 26th	Continued in billets. Coys Training.	
"	Sept 27th	"	
"	Sept 28th	1 officer 250 OR returned from XIV Corps HQ.	Officers 26. O.R. 985
"	Sept 29th 30th Oct 1st	Coys Training.	
"	Oct 2nd	Officers & NCOs "proceeded to FONTAINE LE CAPPY to visit trenches held by 2 R.I.F. with a view to relieving same from them Oct 4/5. Trenches on the whole held several men in places knee and very close.	

Alburay
Cap't May'r

81st Inf.Bde.
27th Div.

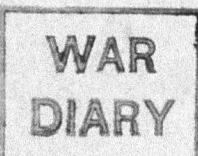

2nd BATTN. THE GLOUCESTERSHIRE REGIMENT.

OCTOBER

1915

Army Form C. 2118.

WAR DIARY
or
INTELLIGENCE SUMMARY.
(Erase heading not required).

Instructions regarding War Diaries and Intelligence Summaries are contained in F.S. Regs., Part II. and the Staff Manual respectively. Title pages will be prepared in manuscript.

Hour, Date, Place.	Summary of Events and Information.	Remarks and references to Appendices.
HQ HORCOURT Oct 3rd	Continued in billets. Received orders to return R.1 Fontaine in FONTAINE-Le-CAPPY so as 113 O O Nov 5 attached.	
b. Fontaine HQ. FONTAINE la CAPPY Oct 4th	Batt. marched out of billets HORCOURT ABP 5-STAM. Route via NERICOURT- 2nd Jordan 4 mile S of FRISBY-CHOIGNES to FONTAINE lu CAPPY arriving 9 AM when battalion halted for breakfast (bivouac). Commenced returning at 10 AM. Transfer F1. F2. G1. G2 taken over complete from 2. R. Buck Fus 1 pm. Very quiet during the day except for a little arr. firing from artillery. Guns nightly occasional shelling of Trench in vicinity. Trenches F1, F2, G1 full of injured (shelled by French) and bodies were buried by German. Post of R were in the Trenches in groups to remove. The ground between the hill a desert with craters of exploded shells, in some cases on top of another, a memory to ourselves. The front Trenches are pretty & require a lot of working on. G1 quite in good front.	Strength Officers 40 Other Ranks 1008 Casualties Lt R.M. Greenshurst wounded b.m. though hung
" Oct 5th	At 7.35 AM enemy exploded a mine under right of G1. (PAYAN) No damage a no casualties. At 8.11 AM enemy exploded another mine under left of F.2. No damage no casualties. To west of the mine nearly to add to mine of craters at PAYAN between ones the lines. At 2.15 PM we exploded "A" mine - succeeded in breaking in enemy sap & gallery. A little shelling in the afternoon. Little sniping during the night, good shot of men during the day, unexpectedly. Trenches very muddy.	Casualty No 16387 Pte Dentford wounded No 9763 Pte Say B. "
" Oct 6th	All quiet during the morning. At noon enemy started shelling our front line and support line of G1, F3, now Horctan and (?) trenches. They kept the bombardment up till about 5 pm when the shell effort. At 4.5 PM enemy exploded a mine near AP PAYAN. Crater luckily not to our front on the damage was done. At 6.10 PM we exploded a counterbalanced mine from TOUFCU near home. A considerable amount of 5. b.(?) by the enemy about 8 AM. At 9-5 enemy exploded a mine about 30 feet of front crater. No casualties & no damage. F2 a G1 got strong fence of pm H.P now went H.M. to west of am. At 9.30 PM the was a bit in G1. His smoke bombs were reps on the back of F2. He rerlipped by the 131 Batty extending, cutting.	Casualty Nil
" Oct 7th	At dawn enemy were seen on edge of new crater. They were shot at & they refused back. There was considerable enemy of pm tic bomb throwing & artillery. They failed to do any great damage. During front 24 hours our sappers have not been able to undertake serious documentary from 12 galleries (?)...	AW... Capt 13th N.Q.R.

Army Form C. 2118.

WAR DIARY
or
INTELLIGENCE SUMMARY.
(Erase heading not required).

Instructions regarding War Diaries and Intelligence Summaries are contained in F.S. Regs., Part II. and the Staff Manual respectively. Title pages will be prepared in manuscript.

Hour, Date, Place.	Summary of Events and Information.	Remarks and references to Appendices.
In Trenches H.Q. FONTAINE les CAPPY	Enemy's artillery fairly active all fronts being continually annoyed with whizzbangs and trench m[ortars]. For this we replied to by our artillery. Shelling Rhen[anus?] Trench in very slow rather an unpaing [sic] by the enemy. Been much enemy aerial activity working between RAVEN corner & FILIPPI Corner, and were continually kept in by our [anti aircraft?]	Casualties nil.
H.Q. CROIGNOLLES 7th		
8th	At dawn it was seen that enemy had dug a trench between RAVEN corner & FILIPPI corner. At 10 P.M. 1 A&S.H. started to observe with a trench. Relief complete by no[on]. Relieved by Argyll Rams at CROIGNOLLES & WHA.	Casualty No. 1109 Pte Gordon G[?] wounded.
H.Q. 9th	Coaches in W.H.B. British batty. Corps clearing up.	Major Turnbull joined Regt.
10th		
11th	Check paraded 10.15 A.M.	
11th	Received orders to W./T.[?] 1 A&S.H. in same trenches to move on 10 A.M. Following in a charge of Pres. Trenches. In contrast to the flat monotony of the area was the corner of France (The ARMENTIERE SALIENT) This country is undulating and wooded Comparatively thickly. The soil is thick with a few strips of clay and sand and again moist. The 2 last being bad for a much-postponing party of all sorts in the wet weather. The Lept (Trench G.I) and extreme right (F.I.) to be on now grounds but the 2 [?] Under Trenches should light. These Trenches had been occupied by the French, before the 27 Div took them over, and as usual they had made very little effort to maintain the strength on the comfort of the line. The Trenches being particularly dilapidated. Rough the communication trench was nearly up to the standard G.2 is about 4000-6000 yards from the enemy and consists of living traverses of any size. The right portion runs up to PMS CONNUN on overall worked, towards the proper of which from the first time A.S.I. [?] and with a unasailable fracture of Trench I must place than a mere shanty. Line 3. was of them probably traversed or with strong enemy parapets. The trench is entered from the enemy clearly discover and entirely opposite the enemy Trench from here to the [?] reached PAYAN order and by 30 yds uprights in the [?] ten of centres says an even Cab at some in the ravine trench. This [?] under PAYAN and from here to the right the section Trench is long of a kind of anomie. Says an even to but it is hopeful for the right the sides of which to the bottom of about 70 feet in width it one was of clear was tracts. At night like the top of a narrow embankment of the Goats hole into here used for it its water, and for the first that past of the Trench was established by the GRAMSI: Further wind for the right the enemy and staffs which our impresent anaging staff or the entirely superseding the PIE taking this not part of the Trench was completed it may 20 by them rig from P.I FILIPPI is a similar trench partly made of well. This is him in a very stiff earth, if any strengthening worked or breakdown the Battn. has a field down in south presses to be mostly plates. Inhabited parades as labelled from the enemy in pulling 3 [?] Interval between Trench 2 Front Section be placed through parades dead ground.	Strength Officers 28 O.R.s 999 [signed] W Wiseon [?] Capt Adj 2 G.H. The last Platoon to [?] the 15th [?] the Grenadiers, [?] held by Batts 2000 yards, with seven

Army Form C. 2118.

WAR DIARY
or
INTELLIGENCE SUMMARY.
(Erase heading not required).

Instructions regarding War Diaries and Intelligence Summaries are contained in F.S. Regs., Part II. and the Staff Manual respectively. Title pages will be prepared in manuscript.

Hour, Date, Place.	Summary of Events and Information.	Remarks and references to Appendices.
In Trenches 12.10.15. FONTAINE to CAPPY	Batt relieved 1 A & S.H. in Trenches F.1. F.2. G.1. G.2. R & L.of captain by 11:30 AM. Batt having moved off by Platoons from CHUIGNOLLES at 9 AM. Very quiet day. Practically no shells only odd shots by Snipers.	Casualties NIL Sick 5 (2 natives)
" 13"	At 2 AM after heavy approach enemy started hooting and rifle grenading our Septembre in the FILIPPI Craters. Is unharmed & replied with Mills bombs. About 2:30 AM they stopped and after having the last word we also started again. We opened with bombs and French mortar throwing 32 lb bombs. At 2-00 AM they stopped and after giving them 10 min's some of them we also stopped. Nearly all the enemy's bombs burst over our Septembre and short of the main firing line. We had 3 wounded including 1 very slight. The remainder of the day the enemy were very quiet, only the ordinary sniping. Very quiet night.	Casualties Grenadier Coy No 9058 Pte Clayton " wounded No 7677 " Banfield C Coy " No 8640 " Steven C. Coy "
" 14"	During the night enemy strengthened their wire opposite FILIPPI Craters. A little artillery firing during the day from both sides. About 3 p.m. large German battalions came over our lines. Their was biggest aeroplane seen up yet. Enemy Transport made a lot of noise in FAY & DOMPIERRE between 6 p.m. & 10 p.m. Very quiet night. Thick Fog	Casualties NIL
" 15"	Very thick fog which lasted about 10 AM. Very quiet day only occasional shots to sustain and artillery & rifle shots.	N.I
H.Q. CHUIGNOLLES 16"	Enemy put a few whizz bangs behind HQ of Gr and support line BOIS COMMUN about 10 AM. Then stopped shortly our guns replied on their trenches. Returned by 1 A & S.H. Relief completed by 12-20 AM. Batt marched back to billets CHUIGNOLLES in Bangors Remnant. Draft of 22 arrived from England.	No 8873 L Cpl Turnbull H.G. wounded Strength officers 28 O.Ranks 1020

WAR DIARY
or
INTELLIGENCE SUMMARY.

Army Form C. 2118.

Hour, Date, Place.	Summary of Events and Information.	Remarks and references to Appendices.
A.Gr. CHUIGNOLLES 14-10-15	L. & Lts. Church Parade to Att. Major R.L. Roundly appointed 2nd in C of 14th Hampshire. Finding 200 men for working party on Trenches strong U-1	Sick from 14th Oct to 17th Oct Officer Ranks 42.
" 16.10.15	L. billets. Cleaning up & tacking off roads to Karrin trenches.	
" 19.10.15	"	
L. Trenches HQ CAPPY 20 Oct. FONTAINE les CAPPY	Relieved 1 A.&S.H. in Trenches F1, F2, G1, G2. Relief completed by 11-30 A.M. Very quiet day handing a shot fired. Suspect a mine up to S13. At 9-15 PM No. 16371 Pte Brett A Coy wounded. Enemy threw over some bombs at Noire PEVAN Crater by reported to has Died of wounds 23rd and enemy went at 10pm. Hearing quite right. Paced at AMIENS.	
" 21 Oct.	Thick fog & very quiet morning. Have seen to Lihen French are returning 27 D.v. in this sector last 23rd. Enemy big guns at night. Trenches in our left taken over by Me French from 22 Div.	Casualties Nil
" 22 Oct.	Enemy snipers very busy in the only enemy opposite FILLIPI. German Parapets had over from our right near 6 left front and was engaged by British Rapid we with M.G. which seemed in German place being brought down on enemy's line in direction of ERNSE about 30 2 balls from 1-10 pm to 2 pm. Enemy shelled the SOCERIE with 42 Howitzers about 30 2 balls from 1-10 pm to 2 pm. A very bright night. Repaired oriface that Pa. 6-10 will be relieved as French by the Regiment right of 264-2'. (About 10 Art working party of army on near F4Y, M8 Bry opened fire B & A by's what muttered as enemy was brig hit) French officers visited trenches WR. a view to taking over tomorrow. Enemy very quiet during the day. About 8 pm enemy put 3 heavy mortar bombs killed F2. They systemically replaced and M&S M.M. settled any bomber of A 117 How Battery immediately shelled enemy's replay and our M&S scatter any launcher opposite F2. They two the day otherwise a quiet n.pd.	Casualties No 20/15 Pte Pillary B Coy KILLED buried FONTAINE les CAPPY

A.W. Viny Capt
Acy. 2 Glos R.

Army Form C. 2118.

WAR DIARY
or
INTELLIGENCE SUMMARY.
(Erase heading not required).

Instructions regarding War Diaries and Intelligence Summaries are contained in F.S. Regs., Part II. and the Staff Manual respectively. Title pages will be prepared in manuscript.

Hour, Date, Place.	Summary of Events and Information.	Remarks and references to Appendices.
HORCOURT 24 Oct 1915	Very quiet morning. Returned by French Cavalry Regt. Relief was carried out on same principle as we have been doing with 1 A&SH i.e. The returning Battⁿ marches up 5 min interval between Coys & 2 min between Platoons, order of march Coy for F₁ - Coy for G₂ - Coy for F₁ - Coy for G₁ - M.G.s - Stretcher Bearers of Battⁿ HQ. FONTAINE to CAPPY each party picked up Run Guide. The 11 L.F. started at BATTⁿ HQ FONTAINE to CAPPY at 1-15 pm and completed at 3-45 PM without casualties. Battⁿ returned to billets HORCOURT all in comp[le]t[ed] 6-45 PM. Stormed last night.	
" 25 Oct 1915	Received orders to march to BOUES tomorrow (distance 15 miles).	O Ranks 1024
BOUES 26 Oct.	Battⁿ marched out of billets HORCOURT 7-40 AM & Route WARFUSEE - ABANCOURT - VILLERS - BRETONNEUX - le Pt BLANGY Cantt - le Pt BLANGY Cantt to camp in N.W. BOUES (distance 15 miles). Only 4 men fell out. Battⁿ all in camp by 2-45 PM. Copy of march attached.	Stormed Officers 29
SEUX 27 Oct.	Battⁿ marched out of camp BOUES 10-15 AM. Route St FUSCIEN - DURY - SALEUX - GUIGNEMICOURT- BOVELLES to billets in SEUX (distance 14½ miles). 8 men fell out near SALEUX. Battⁿ all in billets 6 pm. Men had dinner on road.	
" 28th Oct	Continued in billets. Grenadier Coy "works out" following system adopted (1) Battalion Grenadier. 1 officer (Lt A R Brown) 2 Sergeants & other ranks. (II) Company Grenadiers. 1 NCO and 8 men per platoon. The Grenadier officer is reponsible for training of all grenadiers.	
" 29th Oct	Very wet day. Coys rout marching, entrenching & chemin ration drill.	
" 30 "	do	
" 31 "	do	Sick from Oct 24th to Oct 31st:- 1 officer 12 O.R. A.W. Curry Capt Adjt 2 Grenadier R

www.ingramcontent.com/pod-product-compliance
Lightning Source LLC
Chambersburg PA
CBHW081444160426
43193CB00013B/2375